BEACH BLANKET
BABYLON

A Hats-Off Tribute to San Francisco's
Most Extraordinary Musical Revue

JANET LYNN ROSEMAN

CHRONICLE BOOKS

SAN FRANCISCO

Library of Congress Cataloging-in-Publication Data:
Roseman, Janet Lynn.
    Beach Blanket Babylon : a hats-off tribute to San
Francisco's most extraordinary musical revue / by Janet Lynn
Roseman.
        p.   cm.
        Revue created by Stephen Jay Silver.
        ISBN 0-8118-1699-0
    1. Beach Blanket Babylon.   2. Revues—California—San Fran-
cisco—History and criticism.   I. Silver, Stephen Jay.   II. Title.
ML1711.8.S2R67 1997
782.1′4—dc20
                            96-42337
                            MN   CIP

Book design by Brenda Rae Eno
Printed in Hong Kong
Cover design based on the commemorative poster created
    by Michael Schwab
Hirschfeld illustrations on pages 8, 20, 62, 75, 85, and 99 and the
    front flap copyright © Al Hirschfeld. Drawings reproduced by
    special arrangement with Hirschfeld's exclusive representative,
    The Margo Feiden Galleries Ltd. New York.
Illustration page 108 top copyright ©Tom Meyer/
    San Francisco Chronicle
Illustration page 108 bottom copyright © Phil Frank/
    San Francisco Chronicle

Distributed in Canada by
Raincoast Books
8680 Cambie Street
Vancouver, B.C. V6P 6M9

10 9 8 7 6 5 4 3 2 1

Chronicle Books
85 Second Street
San Francisco, CA 94105

Web Site: www.chronbooks.com

DEDICATION

For my Mother, Theodora, to remind her of her magic.

ACKNOWLEDGMENTS

Writing books can be a very arduous and painful
process, but this book was pure delight to research and
to write. Special thanks to the following people who
helped make this project possible and enjoyable: Jo
Schuman Silver, Jay Schaefer, Kate Chynoweth,
Charlotte Mailliard Swig, Ellen Magnin Newman,
Armistead Maupin, Ken Swartz, David Lincoln King,
Val Diamond, Kenny Mazlow, John Camajani, Alan
Greenspan, and Kate Silver. And a very special thanks
to Luci Lussing.

I am grateful to Jo Schuman Silver for entrusting
me with the *Beach Blanket Babylon* files and for her
support and commitment through the project. It is my
wish that Steve would be highly amused while reading
this book.

CONTENTS

IL FAUT DONNER À RÊVER ET À RIRE.

(You must give them something to dream about and something to laugh at.)

—Paul Derval
Proprietor of the Folies Bergère

How do you know when you've found your soul mate?

Steve and I knew instantly—that very special moment when you first connect, when you feel indelibly intertwined and bound together. We both felt and knew it; we became inseparable for the next fourteen years. I always knew that Steve was a creative genius—that was clear to everyone as soon as they saw *Beach Blanket Babylon*—but he was so much more than that. He was generous, he was charismatic, and his wit, warmth, and unique sense of the absurd enriched the lives of everyone he touched. It's been said, countless times by his friends, his family, and those who loved him, that what they loved most was his magnetic energy. You can just feel his intense energy inspiring every moment of his magical creation, *Beach Blanket Babylon*!

—Jo Schuman Silver

Birth of an Idea

Steve Silver was the last, and probably the greatest, of a particular species rapidly disappearing all over the world known as the theatrical genius. His death from AIDS in 1995 left an enormous void that cannot be filled because there just isn't anyone like him. In 1974, when his first *Beach Blanket Babylon* show opened at the Savoy Tivoli, a popular North Beach cafe in San Francisco, little did he know that his zany ninety-minute musical feast would endure for twenty-three years, and then some. Since then, there have been numerous incarnations, each one a pastiche of hilarity, parody, fantasy, triumphant stagecraft, and musicality of the highest order. By temperament, the creator of *Beach Blanket Babylon* was a visionary blessed by the Muses with

an apparently endless imagination. The man who invented the show's signature of outrageously wild and enormous hats could easily hold his own with Lewis Carroll's Mad Hatter from *Alice in Wonderland.*

Beach Blanket Babylon has proven to be a more durable topic of conversation than almost any other San Francisco institution, including the Golden Gate Bridge, the cable cars and the Transamerica Building. A visit to *Beach Blanket Babylon* is not only required of any self-respecting San Franciscan, it's a tradition. Natives know its charms, and it's not unusual for those who dwell in San Francisco to have seen the show ten, twenty, or for some devotees, fifty times. It may be true that one can get by in the world without seeing *Beach Blanket Babylon,* but the question is, Why would you want to?

Silver created an unforgettable, hard-to-describe extravaganza in which sanity is thrown out the window and the images you first see on stage rarely stay as they are. Tables dance, inanimate objects sing, cultural icons swoon and cavort, and anything and everything goes. And those hats! They shine, glimmer, pulsate, and knock you out of your seat. Garbage cans do the cancan, French poodles sing, and the famous San Francisco hat is in itself worth the price of admission. Silver's world was not only made up of fantasy; it was a world of freedom where his wacky, campy, and affectionate spirit ran free.

If we lived in another time or another culture, Silver would have been dubbed the magician of his tribe, conjuring up wizardry and enchantment for his brethren. A master sorcerer, he possessed an uncanny gift for recognizing the public's fancy, and he conjured up just the right elements. Although he did not invent laughter, he certainly found new uses for it, for he knew that humor was the universal balm that would withstand the test of time; and he was, of course, right. Millions of people from all over the world have loved the show for the most obvious reason. It's funny; and, in today's world, laughter is no small commodity.

Silver was a man who defied definition, and describing him as a theatrical producer just doesn't go far enough. The handsome, charismatic creator of *Beach Blanket Babylon* planned, sketched, designed, rehearsed, wrote, chose music for, hired performers for, and otherwise fully orchestrated every last detail of the production. All of his talents would converge in the definitive San Francisco show; and although he is no longer among us, his madcap flair remains.

Beach Blanket Babylon has presented some of the most spectacular theatrical events since the performances in ancient Rome at the Hippodrome. Following that tradition of grand spectacle, Silver has left San Francisco with continuous amusement. In a city where there is something to see, hear, and be entertained by at any hour, travelers (native and non-native alike) eventually find their way to *Beach Blanket Babylon,* mostly because of Silver's remarkable ear and eye for show-stopping talent and gorgeous visual effects.

The old adage, "You can see almost everyone in the world go by if you sit long enough," is actually true in *Beach Blanket Babylon*'s case. Audience members have been in the company of royalty, actors, cult heroes, politicians, models, sports figures, fashion moguls, and legendary dancers. What other show but *Beach Blanket Babylon* would attract the likes of Mary Martin, the Queen of England, Francis Ford Coppola, Jimmy Stewart, Rudolph Nureyev, Tony Bennett, John F. Kennedy Jr., Bob Hope, Calvin Klein, Joe Montana, and Yoko Ono?

Above: *The creator of* Beach Blanket Babylon, *Steve Silver; the man behind the inspired lunacy that has lasted over two decades.*

Silver's epoch was and is *Beach Blanket Babylon* and his spirit still lights up the room at Club Fugazi. In San Francisco, where everything is done in a grand manner, there is a vintage phrase to describe doing up the town—it's called "seeing the elephant." In this case, though, when you come to San Francisco to see the elephant with *Beach Blanket Babylon* on your list, watch out, for that is a distinct possibility. Thanks Steve.

—*Janet Lynn Roseman*

CHAPTER ONE

The Early Years

STEPHEN JAY SILVER WAS WHAT ONE COULD AFFECTIONATELY CALL A "CHARACTER" IN THE BEST SENSE OF THE WORD. IN HIS VIVID IMAGINATION, EVERYTHING AND ANYTHING WAS POSSIBLE, AND THE RECORD-BREAKING SUCCESS OF HIS CREATION, *Beach Blanket Babylon*, IS PROOF POSITIVE THAT DREAMS CAN COME TRUE. WHO BUT STEVE SILVER COULD PARLAY A GROUP OF LOCAL STREET ENTERTAINERS, GARBED IN FRUIT-SALAD HEADPIECES AND WACKY COSTUMES, AND SINGING MUSICAL HITS FROM BEACH-PARTY DAYS, INTO AN ENDURING SAN FRANCISCO INSTITUTION? BUT IT WASN'T HIS INTENTION TO BECOME A THEATRICAL WIZARD, IT SIMPLY WAS HIS FATE.

POSSESSED WITH BOUNDLESS CREATIVITY THROUGHOUT HIS LIFE, SILVER SPENT MOST OF HIS WONDER-BREAD YEARS PAINTING DESIGNS

ORIGINAL PASSPORT PHOTO

WARNING!

If you see these four fugitives from San Francisco in this area during the holiday season you should report immediately to your nearest psychiatrist — because you're nuts brother.

They are on the S.S. Santa Leonore enroute to Panama and Central America and wish you were going along.

Meanwhile all the Silvers — Claire, Lou, Steve, and Roger, wish you a Very Merry Xmas and a Happy and Prosperous New Year and hope to see you soon (for the 1950-1951 season).

Above: *The Silver family possessed a unique sense of humor, and it's easy to see how Steve inherited his parents' penchant for the whimsical. His family's 1950 Happy Holidays card is a case in point.*

Previous: *Steve Silver's street performing group Tommy Hail was literally created during a five-minute car ride. No doubt there is one Tommy Hail walking around who hasn't the vaguest notion that his missing suitcase would be an inspiration to Silver. Silver found a suitcase with the name "Tommy Hail" emblazoned on it and decided to dub his troupe with that name.*

in the basement of his parents' San Francisco home because, for him, art was as essential to his life as breathing in and out. Lucky for him, his parents, Claire and Lou, were not only charmed by Silver's obvious talents, but promoted them. As a youngster, he created countless canvases and even staged parades, much to the delight of his family and neighbors. It was soon clear that he was not like the other children.

His parents' support and encouragement extended into his entrepreneurial days, when he began staging theatricals. His mother, who had an impeccable eye and a flair for design, sewed the sequins on the costumes, cleaned the tables of the clubs where his group performed, and even enlisted the aid of her bridge club members. His father served as his business manager and was responsible for the show's longtime residence at Club Fugazi. Even his younger brother, Roger, a one-time rock composer, helped out with the day-to-day operations of the shows. Family was always important to him, whether immediate or adopted, and his parents' belief in their son's unusual talents was a great gift to him.

It was when Silver was a fine arts major at San Jose State University that he would discover his true niche. His years at college proved to be a fertile testing ground for what was to come. While other students were living in dorms and swigging beer all night, Silver was creating a tableau of enchantment in the old, run-down house he shared with his roommates near the campus. Their home was decorated much like a theater set, establishing a particular mood of whimsy and nostalgia. Using cast-off furniture from neighbors, he filled the house with vintage wicker and lush velvet curtains. He painted the kitchen a screaming, fire-engine red, and each of the bedrooms was painted a stylish black and white. An apothecary jar next to his bed was filled with hundreds of his hand-painted eggs. Those eggs would prove to be his first lucrative business venture, and one Easter he earned $1,800 selling them to the students on campus. The genuine church pews in the living room would later come in handy when he staged his first "event"—a mock wedding, circa 1928, replete with authentic details of that era. The hundred guests who attended knew that this man was not your average mortal.

Nothing was ordinary or too outrageous for him. He took great delight in following his creative voice and had a knack for convincing others to join him in his special brand of lunacy. When he was interested in filmmaking, he often asked his friends to do the most outrageous things; and they always agreed, since no one could refuse Steve Silver.

A man born with theatrical flair, Silver was making performance art years before the term was coined. His art shows at San Jose State were the talk of the campus. In one of his "breakfast shows," he hung his beautifully surrealistic paintings of cows, oranges, and milkmaids in one corner of the art building. Those who wished to attend entered a door marked "Special K"; once inside, they mingled with live chickens sitting among his canvases. For his master's thesis, Silver rented an old bocce court and cleared out debris eight feet deep so he could fill it with 975 feet of fresh grass. To lend greater authenticity, and in order to

Above: *Steve's parents, Lou and Claire, were completely supportive of Steve and his artistic pursuits. During the Rent-A-Freak days, when Steve was beginning his entertainment career, his mother gave more than her encouragement; she not only sewed many of the costumes for the troupe, even her bridge club members were part of the show.*

13

create the perfect setting for his five portraits of children sitting atop ponies, he hauled stacks of hay to the site. On the day of the show, a little old lady played piano off key at one end of the court while a photographer was available to shoot pictures of anyone who wanted to pose on the pony. Over five hundred people attended the show and sipped champagne from jam jars, since he couldn't afford champagne glasses. KQED, a local television station, even showed up to film the goings-on.

Silver loved to stage events, and in those early days of the 1960s he found his talent for creating entertainment. Unlike the many students who were busy liberating their sexual, political, and pharmaceutical consciousness, Silver was liberating his artistic spirit in ways that boggle the mind. At San Jose State, he staged beauty contests with members of the Geritol set and events for his Theta Chi fraternity in order to liven things up. It made perfect sense that his next step after graduation would be the creation of Rent-A-Freak. This odd entourage of more than eighty people offered its unique services to cocktail parties and charity functions. If you think Federico Fellini, Dr. Seuss, and Lewis Carroll, you'll get the idea. His first "freak" was dressed like a ballerina and walked around hugging the walls, oblivious to everyone at the party. After a while, the vacant-eyed dancer collapsed, and six little cotton clouds appeared and carried her out. Silver's phone was soon ringing off the hook with requests from notables to plan an event for them.

Above: *Silver's college days at San Jose State were a lucrative testing ground for his novel ideas. "I used to have beauty contests with little old ladies and stage parties at the fraternity with costumed characters in order to liven things up." Those wandering characters would be the seed for his business, Rent-A-Freak, pictured above.*

His madcap flair for the improbable led him to create (to use the jargon of the day) "happenings." Silver disliked that term. "It implies that I take myself seriously. I'm having a good time, that's all; and I like it when it rubs off on other people." Some of the events that he created in his early days include:

A formal wedding reception set in a flophouse, where guests sipped champagne from brown paper bags amid plaster cupids and garlands of flowers.

The re-creation of a fourteenth-century Spanish monastery, replete with wandering minstrels, for the opening of the San Francisco Opera season.

A birthday bash for the director of the American Conservatory Theater; guests were transported to Golden Gate Park to cavort amongst Isadora Duncan-type creatures and assorted wood nymphs. Elves hidden in the trees tossed strawberries to the guests. The hard-to-please theatrical crowd was enchanted.

Members of the cast, including Steve Silver and Nancy and Roberta Bleiweiss, frolic at a North Beach parade.

Silver always defied the rules of custom, not in an effort to be rebellious but so he could be true to his artistic vision. "I don't know what the rules are," he told one reporter, "I don't like things that are *supposed* to be. And, I'm not interested in doing something someone else has done before." After the success of Rent-A-Freak, Silver was hired by the American Conservatory Theater, first as a prop man and later as a party planner. "American Conservatory Theater asked me to work for them because they were familiar with my weird services. When they asked me what kind of job I wanted, I told them I wanted to have a good time, so they put me in the prop shop." The time he spent at ACT was important, since it gave him access to the technical aspects of theatrical staging and he had free rein to create parties with his own stamp.

In 1970, he was hired to work on the cult movie *Harold and Maude* by Colin Higgins, the author of the book. Higgins had met Silver in the late sixties when they both served as deck hands on a ship bound for the Orient. The filmmakers were looking for an assistant art director, and Higgins offered Silver the gig. The design for the boxcar where Maude (Ruth Gordon) lived was based on the real-life abode of Silver's ninety-year-old Yugoslavian Aunt Vinka. But it was his creation of the cast party to end all cast parties that left both Gordon and her husband, Garson Kanin, speechless. Because of filming delays, the party was not held until after Christmas, but, no matter: Silver wanted a Christmas party with all the trimmings, even if it was March, and that's exactly what he created. He hauled in thousands of pounds of snow, spread it over his parents' lawn, and dotted the landscape with forty Christmas trees. Surgical cotton clouds scurried about the celestial landscape, which was draped in sheets of gleaming black plastic, and an old woman played Christmas carols on an upright piano. It was March! The actress (Ruth Gordon) approached the scene warily, clutching the arm of Garson Kanin, her author-producer husband. Suddenly, out of the darkness, a 250-pound

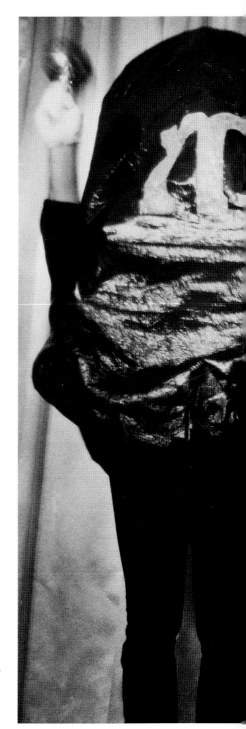

. . . .

Right: *In 1974, during* Beach Blanket Babylon's *earliest run at the Savoy Tivoli, Mary-Cleere Haran sang "Put the Blame on Mame" in a sultry voice wearing a form-fitting black strapless gown. Her satin dress was an exact replica of the dress Rita Hayworth wore in the film* Gilda. *Here she is joined on stage by the dancing M&Ms (Plain and Peanut). Steve is one of those vocal candies.*

Harold and Maude

Ruth Gordon, the star of that inimitable cult classic *Harold and Maude*, had a great effect on Steve Silver. Although she was decades older than the young assistant art director, they were kindred spirits with a joyful zest for life. Gordon attributed her success to her attitude believing that "anything was possible," a world view that Silver heartily embraced.

Clockwise from top left: *Colin Higgins, Bill Lanese, Steve Silver, Nancy Bleiweiss, and Bud Cort*

For instance, even at the age of eighty-seven, when she was filming her last movie, *Maxie,* she insisted on doing her own stunt work and rode a motorcycle for the first time in her life. Just listen to her words of wisdom: "I never face facts; I never listen to good advice. I'm a slow starter, but I get there." When she left her home in Massachusetts setting her sights on being an actress in New York, her father gave her a year's tuition to a drama school, fifty dollars' spending money, and an old spyglass. Telling her that she would be in and out of hock shops all of her life if she was going to be an actress, he wanted to give her some leverage. Gordon sold plenty in those shops, but never that spyglass.

Harold and Maude author Colin Higgins, above, was another example of local-kid-makes-good. While attending UCLA's film school, he wrote the screenplay for *Harold and Maude* and worked as a chauffeur and poolsweeper for the producer of *Spartacus*. Higgins got up his nerve to tell his employer's wife that he had written a screenplay, and she made sure her husband saw that it was seen by the right people. Bob Evans would make it eventually, hiring Hal Ashby to direct since Higgins was too inexperienced.

female cherub in pink tights rocketed toward the couple on high-topped red roller skates. "Can I get you a drink?" asked the angel. "Somehow," said Kanin, smiling at his wife, "I always knew it would be like this."

Silver's next business venture, with the unlikely name Tommy Hail, was born almost by accident. Who except Silver would have thought that a suitcase with "Tommy Hail" on it would be the start of something big? One evening Steve and his friends the Bleiweiss sisters noticed a guitar player on the street who was performing for an admiring and financially appreciative crowd. Silver told his companions, "Let's go back to my house, put on the costumes I have from Rent-A-Freak, and see if we can make enough money to go down to Hollywood." The trio donned costumes and Steve immediately wrote a script for the newly formed group, Tommy Hail—and another successful entertainment event was born.

The outrageously clad group—Roberta Bleiweiss dressed as Santa Claus, her sister Nancy as Carmen Miranda, and Silver attired

as a Christmas tree—crooned ditties like "Close to You," "Where the Boys Are," and "Someday My Prince Will Come." They collected eighty-five dollars in an hour and a half; after only a few weekends entertaining on the street, Tommy Hail drew huge crowds of more than four hundred people. "People were standing on mailboxes and car bumpers and shimmying up lampposts in order to see the tap-dancing Christmas tree. But the main thing was that the people were enjoying it as much as we were." One evening, six paddy wagons drove up to their performance ready to arrest the group because someone had reported that people with crazy costumes were roaming the streets. This was Silver's cue to take the next step; flushed with success, he convinced the proprietor of the North Beach bar and restaurant, the Savoy Tivoli, to let him put on

Above: *The on-stage antics of the cast members in the early years had the Savoy Tivoli regulars hanging from the ceiling like bats. Costumed as a Christmas tree, Silver sometimes appeared on stage with matching red and green maracas which held glass beads that would fly out at the unsuspecting audience. Roberta Bleiweiss is clad in the Santa Claus outfit.*

Above: *Nancy Bleiweiss, the dark-haired, saucer-eyed comedienne, met Silver when he was the house manager for the San Francisco club the hungry i. When he was tearing tickets at the door, Nancy Bleiweiss and her sister, Roberta, asked if he could sneak them into a performance of* Dames at Sea. *He willingly complied. For fun one evening Silver asked Nancy to sing a song from the show and he told her, "Someday, I'm going to produce a show and you'll be my star." And he kept his word.*

a production called "A Valentine's Show." It was a hit. Silver renamed the show *Beach Blanket Babylon* and on June 7, 1974, a San Francisco institution was born.

The goofy summer musical was anything but predictable, and it took San Francisco by storm. Charlotte Mailliard Swig, who would become San Francisco's chief of protocol (and who was one of Silver's earliest fans and a great friend) offered her help to assure the show's success. When the show was ready to open, Silver called her to ask how he could get the press to opening night. Swig reminisces, "At the time I told Steve, 'I have great respect for the press, and you can't just ask the press to do something for you; you have to create something that they want to cover.' He wanted certain people in the press and certain people from the city to see the show. It was my sister-in-law's birthday. Her husband had died that year, and nobody wanted to celebrate her birthday. But I thought it would be a *good* time to celebrate her birthday. I called Steve, and I told him that we were going to have a party and I would bring all these people to his opening-night performance. I invited them to come dressed in what they would wear to their vacation homes, since it was June. These were people who had homes in Napa, Tahoe, or Carmel, and they came as tennis players, sailors, etc. We used beach towels on the tables and I ordered chicken, watermelon, and chocolate covered ants for all these people. Of course the newspaper people did come. That night they blew the lights, because everything was hooked up with orange and yellow extension cords. There was sand on the floor, and they sprayed people's hands with Coppertone. As a surprise, some of my sister-in-law's friends were hula dancers in the show. When people arrived, Steve was still gluing glitter on Glinda the Good's dress. I am sure people didn't know what the heck was going on. I thought it was wacko-wonderful."

When Swig bought out the house at $2.50 a ticket, her friends entered into a world that only Silver could create; the chairs faced a stage outfitted with beach umbrellas, half-buried beer bottles, and a white capped ocean wave, from which the performers entered. Even the crew was part of the zaniness; the lighting man, dressed in swimming trunks, sat at the back of the room on a lifeguard platform. The waitresses wore bikinis, and the ushers wore white *Beach Blanket Babylon* T-shirts and had zinc oxide on their noses. Dressed like French poodles, the musicians were as much a part of the program as the performers.

Silver designed two spectacular costume changes for Nancy Bleiweiss that were precursors to the outrageous attire that the *Beach Blanket Babylon* cast wears today. Her pink satin and billowing tulle fairy gown with its tall plastic-and-rhinestone crown (much like the character of Glinda the Good Witch from *The Wizard of Oz*) and her pineapple hat embellished with life-size paper pineapples and plastic hula girls, worn with a sequined sarong, were monumental architectural designs. *Beach Blanket Babylon* was the zaniest revue that San Francisco had ever seen.

Over the years, critics have tried to decipher the significance of the "Babylon" part of the title, either by recalling the great and crumbled civilization of the same name or by pointing out that Babylon is a euphemism for Hollywood, but to no avail. Silver never admitted that he consciously satirized anything; he was merely having a great time. A tremendous fan of the Frankie Avalon/ Annette Funicello beach-blanket movies, he successfully blended all of the fun of the beach culture without making fun of it. And what merriment it was. A spoof of the Beach Boy music and surfer movies, the zany hats, outrageous puns, caricatures of popular entertainers, and terrific performances were already evident even in the early productions. Silver had the pulse of what audiences were looking for, and even though he invested virtually all he had on the first production, *Beach Blanket Babylon* would soon be in demand. He accounted for its success years later by saying, "It's pure escapist entertainment. God knows there's enough depression, what with the newspapers and TV constantly exposing the tragic side of life. Our show has no heavy message, nothing earthshaking or profound—just a good time. That's what people want in entertainment . . . a good time."

Above: *Dressed in oceans of white tulle, Nancy Bleiweiss was the perfect Glinda the Good Witch from the* Wizard of Oz.

Steve drew every element of the show, and he would use these sketches to explain to the cast what their character would be like. These examples show his earliest sketches and the end product in full Beach Blanket Babylon splendor on stage.

A JOYOUS HOMECOMING

by Stanley Eichelbaum

San Francisco Examiner

Monday, June 30, 1975

Who said the fifties were dull? Well, you might think of it as the Ripsnorting Decade when you see Steve Silver's delightful new revue, "Beach Blanket Babylon Goes Bananas!" which opened last weekend at Club Fugazi Hall, at 678 Green Street.

Producer-director Silver has a special affection for the fifties, as he's shown in previous editions of "Beach Blanket Babylon," a mad and merry musical home brew, which has become something of a North Beach fixture.

The new show is true to form in that it stomps through the fifties, spilling over here and there into other decades, as it lets loose a wild, inanely funny explosion of camp nostalgia.

Though Silver's troupe had a joyous and tumultuous homecoming, which attracted old friends by the score, a number of new faces have joined the show to flesh it out. There are ten lively performers in this more populous expanded "Babylon."

Silver, who also designs these productions, has given Nancy Bleiweiss a couple of outrageously over-done new head-dresses for her Carmen Miranda parody, one of which is a Carmenized Dolly Levi chapeau for a "Hello, Dolly" finale.

Among the more enjoyable moments are Glenda Glayzer's blue-haired, rousingly belted rendition of "Am I Blue?" and Lynn Brown's gorilla striptease to "Night and Day." Philip Tobus, Fran Moitoza, Bill Kendall, Jim Reiter, Roberta Bleiweiss, and Kirk Frederick also make diverting contributions under Silver's and Michael Biagi's spirited co-direction.

No show in town provides a more generous helping of pure, unadulterated pleasure.

The show was so successful that it didn't escape the notice of a Texas notable, Doug Brinkman, who persuaded Silver and what Brinkman mistakenly termed "The Babylons" to close down for two nights in order to appear in Houston at The Alley Gala, one of the town's liveliest charity events. This would be the first show outside of San Francisco, but not the last. Texas has high hats and a sense of humor, but the swells there had never seen a show with Glinda the Good Witch singing "Where the Boys Are" backed up by the Plain and Peanut M&Ms, a French poodle band, and Bleiweiss's hilarious spoof of Carmen Miranda—complete with her four-foot pineapple headdress—singing "I's like to be-e-e in Ameri-ee-ca" backed up by a maraca-shaking Santa Claus and a Christmas tree. Silver, it should be noted, arrived in Houston in costume as a Christmas tree, which gave the airport security officials some pause.

Below: *Silver's attention to detail was legendary. He was involved in every aspect of the* Beach Blanket Babylon *performances, which is one of the reasons for the show's success. "In the early days I did all of the hats. I would design them and make them. I don't know how to sew, but I would glue them together, stick things in Styrofoam, and pray and cross my fingers they would hold together."*

The success of the run at the Savoy Tivoli led Silver to stage the production at the Olympus Club, which was billed as "America's Bisexual Showplace" (remember this was San Francisco in the 1970s). Although the club catered to a gay audience, it wasn't limited. *Beach Blanket Babylon* shared the bill with Charles Pierce, the drag impressionist, but it stole the show and the reviews followed suit. Pierce closed and *Beach Blanket Babylon* went on to play for two months. Don McLean praised the Olympus Club show in the *Bay Area Reporter* saying, "I reviewed *Beach Blanket Babylon* when it played the Savoy Tivoli and said, at that time, it was *the* show in the city. Now it is at Olympus, and it's still the best show in town, even better than before. The 90 minutes zip by far too quickly."

The next step for Silver was to his permanent home at Club Fugazi.

THEY'RE ALL GOING "BANANAS"
by John Wasserman
San Francisco Chronicle
July 11, 1975

"Beach Blanket Babylon Goes Bananas," the spirited heir, if not sequel, to "Beach Blanket Babylon," is a very funny comedy revue—again, built on nostalgia—with some highly talented musicians, singers and hoofers, bright and imaginative costumes, backdrops and props, and a producer-director-designer, Steve Silver, who is little short of genius.

The show opens with a quartet of musicians, dressed, logically enough, as sheep, playing, "Yes, We Have No Bananas," followed by the appearance of the famed Planter's Peanuts Peanut singing, "Stardust," followed by three lads in Bermuda shorts rendering "Twilight Time," followed by two mobile M&Ms who join "Stardust," followed by three young ladies who break into "Stairway to the Stars," followed by the first grand entrance of Miss Bleiweiss attired in a pink prom gown covered with stars, a wand and a mammoth, diaphanous pink crown—yes, it must be said, the Fairy Godmother—and singing "California Here I Come."

Fugazi Hall, the 678 Green Street location of "Bananas," jammed to the rafters (on a Wednesday night, yet), simply erupted. And that was the pattern for the no-intermission, 95-minute (including a solid ten minutes of encores of one kind or another) show; nine singers appearing and reappearing in different vestments, singing songs of the Old West ("Tumbling Tumbleweed") and the New West ("Dedicated to the One I Love").

Opposite: *Cavorting on a local beach, the tiny cast of* Beach Blanket Babylon *had little idea when this picture was taken that the revue would become so big.*

26

Charlotte Mailliard Swig:

The Beach Blanket Babylon Poster Girl

he never said no to any of the crazy things I asked him to do; and I asked him to do a lot of things." Kindred spirits, Swig's friendship with Silver was another prototype of pure pleasure, and each of them took great joy in surprising the other with their fancies. Birthday celebrations were often the focal point for their mutual *joie de vivre*. On one birthday occasion, Swig arranged for a birthday party atop the cupola of San Francisco's City Hall. To get there, they had to walk up winding stairs and one place on the climb was declared a "Cardiac Arrest" stop. Once atop the building, they discovered violins, crystal service, balloons,

Silver's best friend, Charlotte Mailliard Swig, had her form immortalized on many posters and programs for *Beach Blanket Babylon* [after she agreed to pose for him as his favorite poster girl.] The lithe and gorgeous form you see on the *Beach Blanket Babylon* programs are all modeled on the results of that one afternoon photo shoot held at Club Fugazi. "When he asked me to pose, I did it and it was great fun. I would do anything he asked, and

and a catered dinner, all arranged by Swig. What made this celebration even more unique was the fact that Silver was terribly afraid of heights and in an effort to cure him, Swig reached for the stars. On another birthday occasion, she took him up the South Tower of the Golden Gate Bridge and arranged for a plane to fly by with a banner bearing the message, "Steve, you have reached new heights."

Swig and Silver were the perfect match in the can-you-beat-this department. Swig, along with plenty of her friends, once surprised Silver in the early morning. Silver was known to sleep much later than the early-to-rise Swig. Playing a melange of loud instruments, Swig and her friends created a cacophony of sounds to wake him up. In return, Silver surprised his gal-pal on her fortieth birthday by bringing her to Cyril's, the restaurant beneath Club Fugazi, where he had ordered her favorite dinner of hamburgers and french fries—and had painted her face into the nightclub's wall mural. For dessert, Silver had Swig place her hands in cement in front of the club, Hollywood style, where they remain.

The pair collaborated on a number of events serving San Francisco including a 1975 Valentine's Dance at the Palace Hotel for the San Francisco Museum of Modern Art. They carefully orchestrated a candy-kiss room; a room called "Heaven," were they had placed the pearly gates; and a Cloud 9 table, where a group of people ate white mashed potatoes all night. One benefit of being Silver's pal was that Swig was often able to wear some of the costumes and hats. On one occasion, she wore the Carmen Miranda hat; and on another *Beach Blanket Babylon* occasion, she attended dressed as an Italian table with French bread on her head. But it was their work together arranging for Queen Elizabeth's visit to San Francisco in 1983 that they were both most proud of. "Steve always had a wonderful way of knowing just how far to go. He was always on the cutting edge and had such great taste and impeccable timing. He had the great ablity to know what people wanted to see and how long their attention span was. He always knew when something was in good taste, and he was always sensitive to other people's feelings. He cared about people, and he cared about San Francisco. I miss him. Now, when I plan events, I sometimes say, 'Let me get it right, Steve.' "

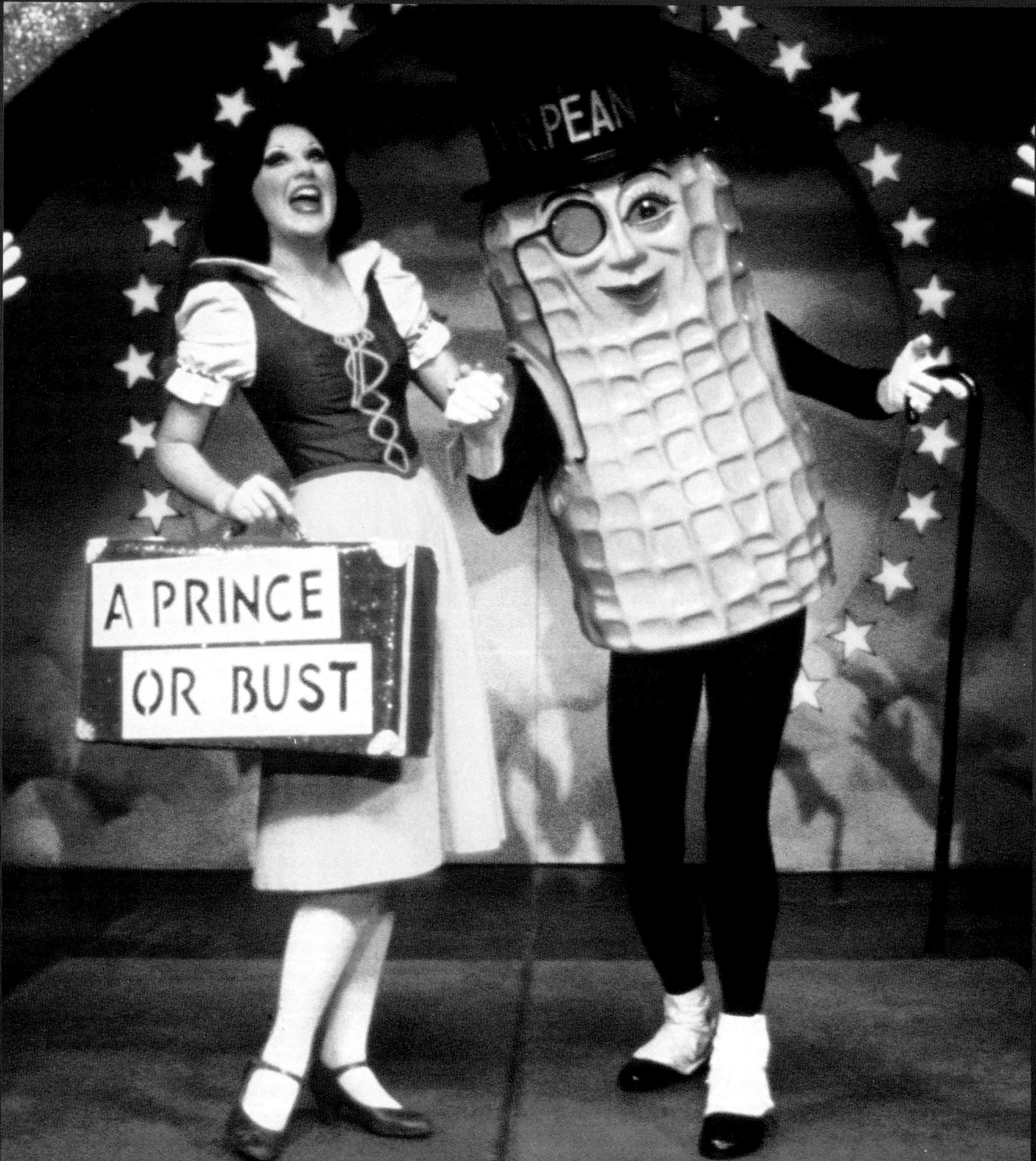
A PRINCE
OR BUST

CHAPTER TWO

Taking Off

SOME PEOPLE (NOT THOSE COMING TO SAN FRANCISCO, OF COURSE) HAVE ONLY THE VAGUEST AND ELEMENTARY NOTIONS OF WHAT CONSTITUTES A GOOD TIME; BUT IN THE CITY THAT IS KNOWN FOR GOOD TIMES, STEVE SILVER'S *Beach Blanket Babylon* FIT RIGHT IN. AN ENDURING VALENTINE TO THE CITY HE LOVED SO MUCH, THE SHOW KNOCKED THE SOCKS OFF CRITICS, TOURISTS, HIGHBROWS, AND NATIVES ALIKE. IN FACT, BY 1977, *Beach Blanket Babylon* WAS SO MUCH INGRAINED AS AN ASPECT OF "MUST-SEE" SAN FRANCISCO THAT THE INCOMING FRESHMAN CLASS AT MILLS COLLEGE WAS REQUIRED TO ATTEND AS PART OF ITS ORIENTATION TO THE BAY AREA.

LIKE THE PROGRAMS IN ANCIENT ROME AT THE HIPPODROME, WHERE LIFE-SIZED SHIPS, HANDSOMELY CLAD GLADIATORS, AND GORGEOUS BEAUTIES ENTERTAINED THE MASSES, *Beach Blanket Babylon* WAS OUTRAGEOUSLY

Above: *Herb Caen, the King of three-dot journalism and the Pulitzer Prize–winning* San Francisco Chronicle *columnist, wrote in 1975, "Everything you've heard about* Beach Blanket Babylon Goes Bananas, *the revusical at Fugazi Hall in North Beach, is true, doubled and redoubled. It's a grand slam; fast, funny, and campy. Meanwhile, be happy, and even happier if you can get into the damn place; the show is sold out a week in advance, and will probably stay that way through the New Year . . . And if you think that I'm feeling humble because* Beach Blanket Babylon Goes Bananas *became the biggest hit in town without so much as a mention in this space, you are right."*

entertaining. Following that tradition of grand spectacle, Silver's show has given San Francisco continuous entertainment and then some. In a town where there is always something to see, hear, eat, and be amused by, travelers and natives usually find their way to a *Beach Blanket Babylon* performance. When "Streets of San Francisco" star Michael Douglas and his then girlfriend, Brenda Vaccaro, attended, they loved it and partied with the cast after the show.

Retitled *Beach Blanket Babylon Goes Bananas,* the show opened on June 27, 1975, at what would be its permanent home, a rococo club in North Beach called Club Fugazi. Silver's dad came up with that brilliant idea, and the club was (and still is) the perfect venue for the show: an elegant old-world nightclub that one might have frequented during the jazz era. At first Silver had doubts about whether he could fill the theater, but he needn't have been concerned. The word-of-mouth success the show had previously established easily brought the fans in. The show was booked for six weeks, and after that engagement sold out, Silver signed a twenty-year lease with the owners of the club, the Italian American Community Services Agency. The rest, as they say, is history. *Beach Blanket Babylon Goes Bananas* was an enormous hit.

According to Silver, Nancy Bleiweiss was a very special talent. "She was hysterical. She had a trick voice and a very special skill with timing. She had these huge eyes, and she was wonderful and just electric with an audience." Bleiweiss seemed able to do almost anything that Silver asked

Right: *Credit goes to Lou Silver for suggesting to his son that* Beach Blanket Babylon *move to North Beach's rococo Club Fugazi. Steve was nervous about filling the 393-seat theater night after night, but he needn't have been concerned since the show earned rave reviews and has regularly sold out ever since.*

Above and Opposite:

Tony Michaels and Nancy Bleiweiss were sensational in their take-off on country western gone bananas. Wearing white ostrich-boa chaps, carrying silver six-shooters and sporting a towering twenty-pound blonde headdress, Bleiweiss was hysterical. Not to be outdone, her partner, Michaels, wore a thirty-gallon hat. Linking arms, they sang a spoof of the famous King and I *song, "Shall We Dance" that was so funny it would have made Yul Brynner smile.*

of her. What really brought the house down was when Silver had her appear on stage coiffed in an outlandish, twenty-pound blonde beehive wig singing "Stand by Your Maa-yann" in a salute to the country-western femme fatale Tammy Wynette. Bleiweiss left the show years afterward to pursue her career. Even though Silver was later involved in a messy legal suit with both Bleiweiss sisters over the origination of *Beach Blanket Babylon* (which he won), Silver, ever the gentleman, was always quick to acknowledge her talents.

After a two and one-half year run of *Beach Blanket Babylon Goes Bananas*, Silver expanded upon his ten-laughs-a-second, fast-moving plot. When *Beach Blanket Babylon Goes to the Stars* opened on June 26, 1978, Silver added his most enduring and best loved character, Snow White. Penny Hamilton played the part, and she parodied the squeaky voiced heroine. Hamilton had been the seven-hundredth to audition, and how she found out about the auditions for the show was pure fate. While appearing in a local production, one of her friends heard her telling jokes backstage imitating the voice of Snow White. He suggested that she try out for *Beach Blanket Babylon* and she did. Hamilton admits that "if he hadn't heard me, I would be probably selling Hallmark cards somewhere in San Lorenzo." (Fairy tales can come true . . .)

In the show, Snow White travels to Los Angeles in search of Prince Charming, and along the way she encounters characters that only Silver could have dreamt up. (This universal theme of looking for love continued in that show and endures in the productions of today.) In Hollywood she ends up at Schwab's as a waitress. The sight gags were endless! Her banana-split headdress, as big as a car, and her dish-topped chapeau were fabulous, as was the hat in the finale, when she wore the *entire* city of San Francisco on her head—it was just over the top. And no one who saw those performances will ever forget Glenda Glayzer's Flying Nun imitation (complete with white robe and flapping veil) or Bill Kendall's caricature of John Travolta. His feverish incarnation of the *Saturday Night Fever* prince singing "Stayin' Alive" in a falsetto voice was in itself worth a ticket. Kendall also played another of the show's stable of characters, Mr. Peanut. Although he had appeared in previous productions, *Beach Blanket Babylon Goes to the Stars* gave him more of an

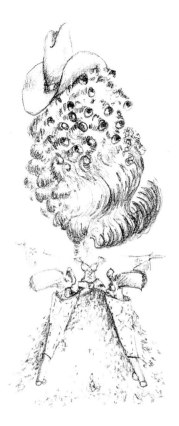

Above: *Shelley Werk's portrayal of Snow White's bawdy, streetwise advisor in Hollywood in* Beach Blanket Babylon Goes to the Stars *earned her critical acclaim. Her "Miss Kitty" chapeau, complete with HOLLYWOOD spelled out, was a scream.*

Right: *Mr. Peanut is one of* Beach Blanket Babylon's *most enduring characters, and Silver even requested sketches from the Planter's Peanut Company so he could duplicate the character's outfit exactly. In various productions Mr. Peanut is frequently ornamented with sequinned hats, gloves, and rhinestone glasses.*

opportunity to showcase his myriad talents. A choreographer and director in his own right before his death from AIDS in 1984, Kendall also produced the popular show *Champagne in a Cardboard Cup*, in San Francisco.

One given in a Silver production is that the characters are more than cardboard cut-outs; they are sweet and funny and wildly entertaining. With the show a success, Silver could have rested on his well-invested laurels, but he didn't; he was always interested in changing the show to make it more enjoyable, more exciting, and more fabulous. He loved to create and recreate. "I love to draw the costumes, and I create through my drawing pad. When I put something onstage that I think is dynamite, I put it there thinking that there is no way this is not going to work; if it gets no reaction the first night, then the second night it is in storage. I love editing because when I start an idea or a concept, I think of every wild idea I can and listen to ideas from anyone else who wants to put energy into it. Let's have no boundaries; let's just create and have a good time."

One time Silver had a good time (make that a *great* time) was in 1980, when he created "Guido's Wedding" in honor of the show's one thousandth performance; it was an early Christmas party as only he could stage it. His hilarious invitations to the mock wedding read, "Steve-A-Silva invitesa youa toa Italiano Kitschmas Aparty ina celebratione ofa 1000th Performansa ofa Beacha Blanket Ababylon Agoza to Astarza." Silver's intent was not to make fun, but to create fun, since he loved everything Italian—the food, the celebration, the music, and the family appeal.

Cyril's, the nightclub below the theater, was often used for special events and parties. The

Above: *Everything is funny in a* Beach Blanket Babylon *production, but Bill Kendall's recreation of John Travolta in his movie* Saturday Night Fever *will long endure.*

Right: *Cyril Magnin, who would do almost anything Silver asked of him, was also hilarious paired with Kendall for one of* Beach Blanket Babylon's *special performances.*

Above: *The "Sundae Hat," a sure-fire crowd pleaser worn by twenty-one-year-old Penny Hamilton, was described by a critic from the* San Mateo Times. *"The audience shouted with delight, yelping and stomping, and even undemonstrative people were seen hollering with unsuppressed glee. The elaborately balanced and executed creations have to be seen to be believed. There is an entire banana split, complete with hot-fudge sauce, melted marshmallow, and a maraschino cherry on top, bordered by those Nabisco wafers we all know and love." The song Hamilton sang wearing her delectable creation was "Sundae My Prince Will Come." At one performance, when Snow White sang it, the Shah of Iran's son was in the audience as a guest of Cyril Magnin. The prince leaned over to Magnin and asked, "Is she singing that for me?"*

Snow White

Steve Silver had an unerring eye for what would make people laugh, and he was an expert at creating extravagant visuals, musical parodies, and other assortments of fun without offending anyone. When he added the character of Snow White, he penned the following notes:

Snow White characteristics:

1. Animated.

2. Naive.

3. Never thinks she's funny.

4. Plays everything totally straight.

5. Voice—high into head/not too quivering—becomes old lady.

6. Walk—small steps and calculated.

Instructions to the actress:

1. Take these characteristics and make them your own.

2. Let the character emanate from within—I want you really to feel and believe what Snow is going through at the time.

Snow White has been an enduring character through the years, and the twenty years haven't changed her looks one bit!

Cyril Magnin

I'm the chief of protocol of San Francisco, and it's my obligation to show our guests the best things in San Francisco. I think that BEACH BLANKET BABYLON *is one of the best things we have. I never let anyone I am responsible for get out of this town without seeing the show.*

—CYRIL MAGNIN

True to his word, the San Francisco mogul saw *Beach Blanket Babylon* over five hundred times. Cyril Magnin, the department store magnate, met Silver during the Savoy Tivoli days and that meeting was a boon for both of them. Although he was more than four decades older than Silver, they had a lot in common and developed an uncommon relationship. Both had a zest for life and shared a positive point of view about the glories of living. According to Magnin's daughter, Ellen Magnin Newman, "My dad had a lot of show biz in his soul. He believed in young people and was accepting and supportive of young talent. He liked to be surrounded by young people with new and creative ideas, and he liked to have fun."

Magnin was an octagenarian who not only adored the theater but wasn't afraid to get into the act. On many New Year's Eve shows, he would take the stage to play Father Time—or even John Travolta. According to his daughter, those appearances were among the high points of his life. But *Beach Blanket Babylon* wasn't the only show in town for Magnin. When he was in his seventies and eighties, he loved to perform at the Lower Mark Bar

at the Mark Hopkins Hotel atop Nob Hill; and when he wasn't at *Beach Blanket Babylon* or attending social events (which bored him), he would sing at the bar. His appearance as the Pope in the film *Foul Play* was another highlight in his show-biz career. Newman remembered, "I think the greatest gift that Steve gave to my father was Colin Higgins and the role in *Foul Play*. Higgins [the director of *Foul Play*] needed permission to use the

opera house for the film. He asked Steve what he needed to do, and Silver told him, 'Go see my friend Cyril Magnin, he can do anything!' When Higgins walked into my dad's office, the director looked at him and said, 'The Pope!' It was terrific to see the joy my father had when he was asked to do a screen test in Hollywood. When he received his check, he was prouder of it than of any other he had ever gotten."

Magnin's hands and feet are immortalized in cement in front of the Club Fugazi.

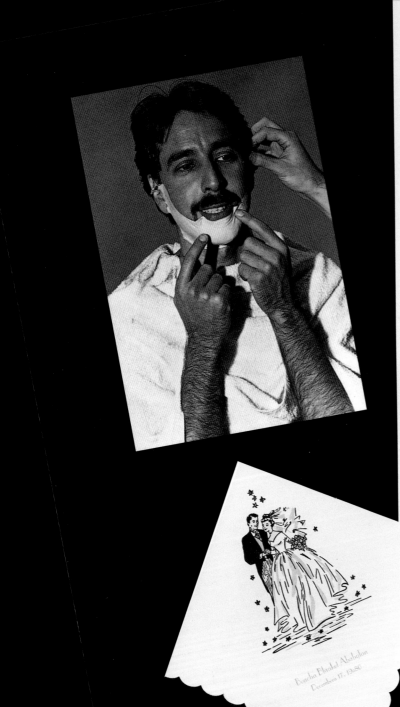

Steve-a-Silver

invitesa youa toa

Italiano Kitschmas Aparty

ina celebratióne ofa
1000ᵗʰᵃ Performansa
ofa
Beacha Blanket Ababylon Agoza to Astarza

ata

Cyril's

Night-a-Cluba
inada base-a-ment ofa Cluba Fugazi
678 Greena Streeta
Sana Francisco

Joina us afora Pasta Buffeá, Cockatailsa
and adancing toa damusic ofa da

Guido Del Rio
Orchestra

anda

Flyinga Ragu Abrothers

Wenza Daya, Decembera 17, 19a80
8:00 p.m.a

Beacha Blanket Ababylon
Decembera 17, 1980

RSVPa 421-4484a

Dressa: Italiano-a-Christmas
Kitsch-a-Optional

This page and Opposite: *Guido's Wedding was one of the most inventive productions Silver ever did; it offered him a rare opportunity to appear on stage as the legendary orchestra conductor, Guido Del Rio. Silver had experience staging fanciful weddings in his early days in college, when he created a mock vintage wedding; but for this one he pulled out all the stops.*

fabulous murals in the club were hand-painted by Silver, and he cleverly depicted many of his friends and San Francisco's highbrows in the scenes, people such as Katharine Cebrian, Cyril Magnin, Wilkes Bashford, Charlotte Mailliard Swig, and Peter Mintun. The name of the club was in honor of Silver's mentor, Cyril Magnin. The guests were greeted by the Salvation Army band singing Christmas carols, while angels on the balcony dropped snowflakes upon the guests below. They had been asked

to come in costume, and they did; Charlotte Mailliard Swig wrapped herself in checkerboard cloth and carried a loaf of French bread, Cyril Magnin wore the Pope outfit that he wore in the movie *Foul Play*, and other guests dressed in equally outrageous costumes. It was impossible to ignore the pungent smells of tomato sauce, and waiters everywhere appeared with meatball delicacies. Silver wanted the wedding to have an authentic old-country feel and based it on a party that his Aunt Vinka would have planned. He even used the jam jars that his guests had sipped champagne from at his first mock wedding back in 1974.

Singers with Italian accents performed, sixteen accordion players sang "Lady of Spain," and the children's choir from a local church sang Christmas carols. But this was no ordinary wedding: how could it be? It was a Silver affair. The guests were guided upstairs to the club, where the theater was decorated with fourteen-foot strands of spaghetti and eight-foot meatballs. The band sat behind huge Ragu jars, and although one wouldn't know by looking at him, Guido Del Rio, the band leader, was none other than Steve Silver. His band members were from a local group with the unlikely name of Pure Trash.

Val Diamond, the queen of the belters, who joined the cast in 1979, and Bill Kendall played the adoring bride and groom. North Beach restaurateurs Fran and Frank Sanchez, the owners of Mama's Restaurant, also participated in the faux ceremony. Diamond may have gotten carried away with the drama when she literally smashed a piece of the wedding cake into her loving groom's face just before they danced the first dance, a rendition of "Hava Nagila," which goes to show that anything and everything is possible at a Silver event.

The individuals who formed the cast of *Beach Blanket Babylon* over the years reflected Silver's unerring eye for talent. Witness his discovery of Val Diamond, who still wows the audience night after night. The entire cast is superb, but there is no doubt that Val Diamond is one of the show's brightest stars. Her renditions of "City Lights," "Coronet Man," and "There's No Business Like Show Business" are unparalleled show stoppers. When the Kennedys (John Jr. and his Kennedy cousins) attended a performance, the hunky and handsome lad singled her out: "I really liked the show. Some of the singers, like the one with the husky voice, boy, can she sing." For almost two decades, Valeria Adriana Maria Francesca Diamond has electrified audiences as only she can.

Always trying to keep the show fresh, Silver added and deleted characters when it was appropriate, striving to be current with the times. For example, in 1985, he did the unthinkable; he replaced Snow White with a "nerdette." Susan Parks, who was playing Snow White at the time, welcomed the change. For inspiration, she studied current and past "nerdettes" like Miss Gooch in *Auntie Mame* and Gilda Radner's Lisa Lubner in "Saturday Night Live." Snow White would later return to *Beach Blanket Babylon,* but not before the nerdette was replaced with the character Dorothy from *The Wizard of Oz*.

★ ★ ★ ★

San Francisco writer Armistead Maupin, author of the successful *Tales of the City* series, wrote dialogue for *Beach Blanket Babylon Goes to the Stars.*

★ ★ ★ ★

44

Silver's celebration of the seventh anniversary of the show—*Beach Blanket Babylon Goes to the Stars and the Beach*—was a dream come true for him. The man who adored the beach-blanket movies of the 1960s in general, and Annette Funicello in particular, had the brilliant idea to stage a Mouseketeer tribute to the queen of the Mouseketeers. He rented California Hall in San Francisco for six weeks, since the Club Fugazi was too small for what he had in mind. Silver had the time of his life; and for that matter, so did Funicello. It was the show that prompted Cyril Magnin to declare of Silver, "He's the Ziegfeld of the '80s: no, I'm wrong, he is greater than Ziegfeld!"

Funicello shunned publicity and led a quiet life at home raising her three children. Except for her role as television spokeswoman for Skippy Peanut Butter, her days in the spotlight were behind her. She was delighted with the invitation, though. A phone call was all it took to get Funicello to agree; and when she saw the show, she was doubly thrilled to be part of it. "It knocked me out. It's one of the best shows I've seen." Once the word got out that Funicello would be the centerpiece for the show, it quickly sold out; even Silver couldn't get extra tickets for the performance. Scalpers were selling seats for $150 each, if you were lucky enough to find one.

On the opening night of *Beach Blanket Babylon Goes to the Stars and the Beach*, the audience didn't need prodding to get into the "Mickey" spirit. Couples wore "I Love Annette" shirts and mouse ears. Even Funicello's parents attended. It was really a sequel to *How to Stuff a Wild Bikini*, Silver-style, and a grand excuse for the audience to bedeck itself in its finest beach attire. Film producer Allan Carr wore a Palm Beach suit with real diamonds. Charlotte Mailliard Swig wore a waving palm-tree hat, and others wore their best "Mickey" outfits. Nine men in their early twenties wore identical sailor hats and checked cotton playsuits with matching gardenias. Inside, the hall was transformed into a Southern-California-dreamin' kind of place, with eleven tons of sand spread on the floor. There were hot dog stands, colorful beach umbrellas, and beach signs, and tourists and locals sat beside die-hard Mouseketeer groupies. The band wore straw hats and Hawaiian shirts.

Above: *Val Diamond, a songstress and comedienne with* Beach Blanket Babylon *since 1979, has talents to match her ceiling-high hats. Her birth name is really Valeria Adriana Maria Francesca, and she frequently cites all of her names when she is on stage in character.*

45

Everyone was waiting for the Funicello tribute, and what an entrance she had! The petite, cult heroine, flanked by six bodybuilders with *Annette* emblazoned on their tank tops, grandly descended a staircase accompanied by the California State Marching Band, a fifty-member choir, and sixty maraca-playing muscle men. Silver even persuaded twenty-five of his high school friends to carry surfboards on stage and engage in some high-kickin'. It was a delight for everyone involved:

Funicello, Silver, and of course the audience. When Annette sang her 1960s hit, "Pineapple Princess," the audience went wild. Then, film clips from her career were shown (remember Frankie Avalon?) and she was interviewed by Mr. Peanut.

The high point of the show was when Mr. Peanut asked her the question, "Who's the leader of the band that's made for you and me?" "M-I-C-K-E-Y M-O-U-S-E," the house screamed back to her, and at that moment the crowd turned into kids again. Funicello was enjoying being on stage again, while Silver was like a kid in a candy store. He spent the evening directing the action and, with a perfect Mouseketeer grin, asked, "Isn't this sick?" (Translation: wonderful.)

Although Funicello's starring role was only a one-night affair, the show continued at California Hall for six weeks before returning to Club Fugazi. Silver added some characters who are still remembered, including an outrageously satirical impersonation of Liza Minnelli singing "Cabaret" clad in black stockings, garter belt, and black-sequined body suit; a dead ringer for Eva Peron singing from "Evita"; a *Chorus Line* imitation; and a Dolly Parton look-alike. Silver concocted many special programs over the years, including tributes to the Queen of England, Cyril Magnin, Mary Martin and Carol Channing, Tommy Tune, and even the politicos in Washington, but that night was his pièce de résistance.

The Queen of Mouseketeerland

Annette Funicello, that queen of beach-blanket movies, was delighted to be coaxed out of semi-retirement when Silver invited her to be part of his tribute to that movie genre. When she appeared in a one-night-only performance of *Beach Blanket Babylon Goes to the Stars and the Beach* at California Hall, the place was converted into the perfect beach environment, and Funicello had a ball. And so did the cast.

A gent of the highest order, Silver always made sure that special attention was given to special people, and Funicello certainly was one of those. Upon her arrival in San Francisco, he made sure she received the Silver treatment. His order for flowers to be placed in her room called for a huge floral arrangement of two dozen long-stemmed roses and two dozen white carnations with a "Welcome to San Francisco" card signed by Silver. The following day, she received a spring bouquet from Silver's parents with the note, "Dear Annette: Good Luck tonight. Break a Leg!"

A dozen red roses and a dozen white carnations arrived from Silver on the day of the show, along with a dozen yellow, red, and white carnations from the cast with the note, "We are really looking forward to tonight."

The Tenth Anniversary

Everybody loves a party, and when the tenth anniversary of *Beach Blanket Babylon* approached in June, 1984, Silver staged the most magnificent prom night a gal and guy could ever want to attend. He wrote the following to the cast in heartfelt appreciation.

It never occurred to me that Beach Blanket Babylon *would enter its second decade of performances. I am grateful that you are all able to share with me in this very special occasion.*

This milestone would never have been possible without the talented, creative people working on the stage and behind the scenes. I wish to express to them my deep appreciation for jobs superbly done.

I lovingly acknowledge my family and dear friends who have tirelessly given their support for all my projects throughout the years. Gratitude also goes to the most beautiful city in the world, my home of San Francisco, for providing the perfect setting for Beach Blanket Babylon.

Our tenth Anniversary would have been impossible without the wonderful audiences and loyal fans in San Francisco, the Bay Area, and across the nation. It is their energy, laughter, and applause that sustains the enthusiasm we all need to continue performing show after show, year after year. To each and every one of you, my love and thanks.

Sincerely,
Steve Silver

Silver arranged another hit presentation for the show's tenth anniversary. Green Street (now called Beach Blanket Babylon Boulevard) was covered with red carpet, and hundreds of white and red balloons formed an arch over the arrival area. Arriving guests, who took seriously Silver's request on the invitations to dress in prom attire, were escorted into the theater by two brass bands: the San Francisco Gay Freedom Day Marching Band and the Riordan High School Band. *Beach Blanket Babylon Goes to the Stars and the Prom* was an incredible success, and it was hard to tell whether Silver, his guests, or the cast members had more fun. White gloves, teased hair, wrist corsages, and tuxes were the order of the evening. Crinoline skirts, taffeta, chiffon, and tulle were the required garb for the women. In the city that loves to dress up, this was a great excuse to dress up fifties style. As one guest commented, "Who'd

ever think a mature woman would dress up like a teenager and dare to show herself in public? But, here I am." Jo Schuman, Silver's great friend (and later his wife), was crowned Queen of the Prom.

Following the tenth anniversary tribute, the new show, *Beach Blanket Babylon Goes to the Stars and the Prom*, ran for eight months. Silver added contemporary characters to the show who gave Snow White romantic advice, including E.T., a hilarious imitation of Dustin Hoffman in *Tootsie*, Boy George, Gandhi, and Michael Jackson. It was a trip down Lunacy Lane very much worth taking.

A few weeks after the tenth anniversary, in July, 1984, *Beach Blanket Babylon* would make theater history by becoming the longest-running musical revue *ever*, surpassing the record set by the long-running *Ziegfeld Follies*. As of June 7, 1997, the twenty-third anniversary of the show, over 8,494 performances will have been given, and more than 3,600,000 people will have enjoyed the merrymaking.

From left: *Lou and Claire Silver, Jo Schuman Silver, Steve Silver*

Chapter Three

Hats On!

The fun factory that is Steve Silver's *Beach Blanket Babylon* is as big a draw as it ever was, and his outrageous headgear is still the star of the show. The house is full every night at Club Fugazi, not only because of the superb entertainment but because the hats have to be seen to be believed. The details of how the hats are constructed and worn on stage remains a carefully guarded trade secret, but the creative process for the hats begins with Silver's sketches. Curiously, he never discussed specifically where his ideas came from, but it was clear that he had an uncanny ability for knowing what makes audiences laugh. He kept volumes of sketchbooks that depicted his designs in great detail, and he added rhinestones, studs, and glitter to

The Christmas Hats:
Santa Would Love It!

Each year, Steve Silver staged a spectacular Christmas show, and the required Christmas Hat finale still brings smiles to the faces of even the most Scrooge-like in the audience. There have been three Christmas Hats created over the years, and as they have evolved, their proportions have grown larger and larger.

Left: *Susan Parks wearing the traditional Christmas hat,* Beach Blanket Babylon *style, during the yuletide season.*

Above and Opposite: *The 1978 San Francisco Hat and Steve's early sketch.*

the drawings, making the costume designs leap off the page. Through the years, hundreds of hats have been created for *Beach Blanket Babylon.* The first headdresses were less than a foot tall. Now they rise almost a dozen feet in the air and require complex electronics and gadgetry. During a performance, each actor in the ten-member cast makes over ten costume changes, and there are over two dozen hats that need to be put on, taken off, and replaced with another outlandish headpiece. With only about twenty to thirty seconds to accomplish this feat, cast members must complete their costume changes with precision and accuracy. These towering crowns are created from a pastiche of glitter, diamonds, fantastic buildings, animals, feathers, dolls, and a host of other everyday items. But who exactly knows how to build the city of San Francisco or the Tower of London on a hat?

The outrageous hat designs that are part and parcel of every *Beach Blanket Babylon* performance were produced by Silver and long-time fellow "mad hatter" Alan Greenspan. The story of how they met is splendid. Before the opening of *Beach Blanket Babylon Goes to the Stars* in 1978, Silver was in a San Francisco record store and one of the cashiers, John Karr, was a big fan of the show. As fate would have it, Silver checked out his purchases at Karr's counter. The pair began to chat, and Silver proceeded to discuss his plans for the new show; as was his wont, he acted out the entire performance! Much to their amazement, a crowd of lucky bystanders saw the producer singing and dancing the show and applauded wildly when he finished. Silver told Karr that he was having problems with the finale and was looking for someone who was skilled enough to execute his ideas for the finale hat. Karr suggested that Silver contact his roommate, Alan Greenspan.

Greenspan possessed the ideal background to help Silver. He had previous experience working at Animation Production Associates, a film studio in New York, and was savvy in animation, retail display designs, mechanical merriments, construction, engineering, painting, graphic design, stained glass design, woodworking, and interior design. He had even worked for the TV show *Mr. Rogers' Neighborhood,*

What would *Beach Blanket Babylon* be without its trademark, the San Francisco Hat that is *always* worn during the finale of the show? Although countless people say that they love to watch the cable car circling the brim of the San Francisco Hat in the finale, it has never occurred. Only the train on the Christmas Tree Hat circles the entire perimeter of the hat. Comparing the San Francisco Hat designs shows how each new design has grown and outgrown previous incarnations.

1979

1981

1986

Opposite: 1997

The San Francisco Hat
at the Opera House:
Opera Never Looked So Good!

The San Francisco Hat that Silver created for the Fol de Rol benefit at the San Francisco Opera was his hat-to-end-all-hats. The stage of the Opera House is the largest in San Francisco, and Silver had to re-create the hat in proportion to that enormous theater since the version he was currently using would be lost on that huge stage. Silver absorbed the cost of creating this mammoth hat, because everyone involved volunteered their talents for the benefit. It was the largest hat ever to appear on stage anywhere! The entire headdress weighs nearly three hundred pounds. The spectacular hat was later displayed at the de Young Museum and inside the San Francisco Centre. At the performance, a proud Lou Silver stands in front of the Opera House with his boy-genius, Steve Silver.

where he created and designed the popular puppet characters Henrietta Pussycat and Sarah Saturday.

Silver and Greenspan are probably best known today for their enormous San Francisco Hat. The original San Francisco Hat, which was introduced in 1977, looked quite different than the current one, but the trademark San Francisco icons were still there—the Ferry Building, the Transamerica Pyramid, Coit Tower, and the cable cars. In the earliest version, Lombard Street was prominent at the front of the hat, and this design was featured on the cover of *San Francisco Magazine* in 1979. Another note of whimsy is that, after the 1989 San Francisco earthquake, the flagpole on the Ferry Building was bent over and the tower clock was set for 5:05 P.M., the exact time of the earthquake. About a year later, the flagpole was straightened since too many people in the audience kept asking why it was bent.

© Al Hirschfeld

Although the San Francisco Hat changed in proportion through the years, it was the gargantuan San Francisco Hat specially made for the San Francisco Opera's Fol de Rol that would be the chapeau to end all chapeaus. During this 1987 benefit performance, Placido Domingo, guest artists from the Royal Ballet of London, and Paul Anka graced the stage, but this hat upstaged them all. The hat was twenty feet wide, eight feet deep and thirty-three feet tall. The brim alone required over sixty yards of taffeta and over two hundred ostrich feathers. This headdress was the largest hat ever to appear on stage anywhere. The hat was so enormous that actress Susan Parks had to be assisted onto the stage by two Groucho Marx characters to support it. Greenspan says, "It was done with smoke and mirrors; I built it in my apartment. The buildings are large enough to walk inside; Chinatown is the size of a phone booth, and the Pyramid is fifteen feet tall and four feet wide at the bottom. Don't try this at home, it's not for casual entertainment. It was my favorite."

Silver would show Greenspan his sketches for the hats he envisioned, and then Alan would construct them exactly as Silver wanted, which was no easy task. Greenspan explains, "Steve would come up with the concept. In 1978, I remember he wanted the Christmas Tree Hat to grow, and he wanted a train to go around it. I added a Santa Claus; as the tree lifts up, it reveals a mechanical Santa Claus." During the early years of the show, the hats were not as large as they are today, and cast members would balance them on their heads. It took a great deal of talent, not to mention balance, since the hats were only pinned into the actor's hair. Later, an elaborate banding system of straps was added to make sure that the enormous chapeaus didn't pivot.

During one notable show, in the early *Beach Blanket Babylon* days, Nancy Bleiweiss wore a Christmas hat that was large and cumbersome. The hat would light up during the finale number, but on one occasion she didn't sing when she was supposed to and remained frozen on stage. The reason? She thought she was being electrocuted due to a faulty wire. There have been a few other sizzling mistakes over the years. When Elizabeth Padilla came onstage in the signature San Francisco Hat, the hat shorted out, and smoke began to billow up; the audience thought it was all just part of the frolic, but the poor woman received quite a jolt of electricity. These mishaps have been few, however, because Silver made sure that each moment of the show was planned and accounted for.

Many of the colossal hats created for the show are truly self-contained stage sets that give new meaning to the term *big-wig*. Reminiscent of the resplendent headdresses of the Folies Bergère in Paris and the Ziegfeld Follies in the United States during the Jazz Age, Silver's idea to create headgear, "Silver-style," was a stroke of genius. Both Silver and Greenspan were frequently called "mad hatters" because of the obvious, but at least they didn't suffer from "hatter's dance," a condition milliners often experienced in the late 1800s. The glue used at that time caused mercury poisoning, a condition that made the poor hat-makers have spasms and sometimes even lose their minds—hence the phrase, "mad as a hatter."

The hats for *Beach Blanket Babylon* are splendid to look at, but what is more amazing is that, each night, they sit atop singers and dancers who are performing show-stopping tunes with huge, bulky objects on their heads—garbage cans, a tray of dishes, an enormous pizza, a lamp post, or an entire skyline. Vocalist Val Diamond gives the actor's perspective: "When you come out wearing really huge hats, you don't kid yourself. You know that it's the hat that you are getting the ovation for. But when you really feel fine is when you've sung some touching ballad wearing something crazy on your head, and you've gotten the audience to stop laughing and listen to you sing, and *then* they give you an ovation. That's when it feels great!"

✫ ✫ ✫ ✫

Cyril's, the nightclub below Club Fugazi, was named after the late Cyril Magnin, department store magnate and one-time chief of protocol for the city. Magnin also has a Royal Box in the theater bearing his name.

✫ ✫ ✫ ✫

Steve's Sketches

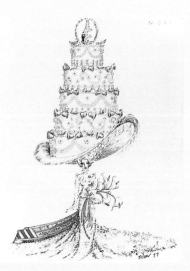

Silver sketched every one of the hats and the costumes for every character in each *Beach Blanket Babylon* production. He used these elaborate sketches to explain his vision of the outrageous to both the cast and the crafts people.

The Washington Hat:
Beach Blanket Babylon Goes to Washington (or tried to)

In August of 1982, Simon Levy, then current manager of *Beach Blanket Babylon Goes to the Stars and Broadway*, was contacted by a representative from the White House— yes, *that* White House—inviting the cast to perform for the then-President and Mrs. Reagan and their guests. The confirmation letter stated, "As I mentioned to you on the telephone, the *Beach Blanket Babylon Goes to the Stars and Broadway* comes to us on the highest recommendation of one of the President's senior aides, and we are delighted that your busy schedule will enable you to make the long trip

East to entertain President and Mrs. Reagan. . . . Everyone here will be delighted to have your talented group entertain at the White House." The original date for the show was September 27, but because of Yom Kippur the date was changed. Rescheduled for September 30, the show would be hosted by the President and the First Lady on the South Lawn of the White House before members of Congress and other distinguished guests.

Needless to say, Silver was in White House heaven, and he proceeded to make plans for *Beach Blanket Babylon Goes to Washington*. Silver created a new edition of his show, including a special finale hat called The Washington Hat. The show was big news for San Francisco, and it even showed up in a Doonesbury cartoon.

On September 21, just nine days before the performance, the *Beach Blanket Babylon* trip to Washington was canceled. The Actor's Equity Association formally protested to White House officials concerning *Beach Blanket Babylon*'s non-union status, and the powers that be decided to avoid any problems that might occur. Silver and the cast were heartbroken, and in a press conference, Silver stated his feelings about the show's cancellation: "To say that all of us involved with *Beach Blanket Babylon* are extremely disappointed not to have the opportunity to perform at the White House would be a gross understatement. As anyone can understand, this was to be a great honor, a wonderful professional and personal experi-

ence and, for all of us, a chance of a lifetime." Silver, who made a point of paying his workers wages that equalled or exceeded local Equity Cabaret minimums, was also proud of the fact that he could offer the cast year-round employment and benefits, which is rare in show business. His press conference addressed these concerns and it was a chance for Silver to explain that "none of us harbor ill feelings toward the President or his staff."

Since he had all of the ingredients for a helluva show, Silver decided to offer San Franciscans a White House edition of *Beach Blanket Babylon*. The show opened on September 30 and ran until October 10, and was billed "The White House Weeks." The show was another enormous success and Silver's political parodies did not go to waste. It was the finale hat that everyone was waiting for, and the cast's depiction of the Reagans was a scream. They appeared

onstage singing "Goin' to the White House and We're Goin' to Redecorate It." Ronnie clutched a jar of jelly beans, and Nancy, of course, wore a red gown displaying a very prominent $20,000 price tag. That price, incidentally, was close to what it cost Silver to build the fifty-pound Washington Hat. On the top of the brim were scale models of the White House, Jefferson Memorial, Washington Monument, and the Capitol Dome, which later opened to reveal a rotating display of American flags. When Alan Greenspan was creating the model for the Washington Hat, he worked using a twenty-dollar bill as a model in an effort to duplicate the building "just so." Even the windows in the building of the White House Hat are green because that's what they look like on the bill. Greenspan only had the twenty-dollar bill to study since it is forbidden to photograph the White House from the air, and he wanted to work from an aerial shot.

The Splendid London Hat:
Fit for a Queen

It might have been the show for the Queen of England during her trip to San Francisco that gave Silver his greatest pleasure. Working with his friend Charlotte Mailliard Swig, the pair had only a few weeks to create the special seventeen-minute segment for the Queen. To make matters more stressful, Silver was also in the midst of an ugly court battle with the Bleiweiss sisters over the creative rights to *Beach Blanket Babylon*. During the court proceedings, Swig and Silver would take notes and pass them to each other on legal pads. As Swig recounts, "Everyone thought we were making extravagant notes for the case, but the truth was, we were writing the show for the Queen of England." During the show itself, the Queen even broke into a laugh (which is not her fashion) when the splendid London Hat opened up to reveal Princess Di and Prince Charles prominently displayed. After the performance, Silver met the Queen, and she broke protocol to whisper in his ear, "I say, we certainly got a lot of telly coverage, didn't we?"

Hats Off to Art!
Beach Blanket Babylon Goes to the Museum

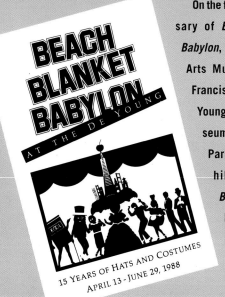

On the fifteenth anniversary of *Beach Blanket Babylon*, one of the Fine Arts Museums in San Francisco, the M.H. de Young Memorial Museum in Golden Gate Park, staged an exhibit of *Beach Blanket Babylon*'s hallmark hats and costumes. From April 13 until June 29, 1988, this artistic salute to the show (and to its creator) presented Silver's gorgeous costumes and headdresses in a prestigious setting. After all, Silver's designs were more than whimsical. They were and are pure artistic expression. Although his first hats and costumes were simply constructed with crepe paper, cardboard and tape, they quickly became more elaborate and outrageous, growing in height, girth, and technical achievement. The de Young exhibit presented all manner of things used in the show, from a sequined Snow White costume to Carmen Miranda headdresses, and a lavish Valentine's Day stage backdrop from the early days of the

show that Silver created entirely with Magic Marker pens. Even the first delicate six-inch flower hat that spawned the first dancing flower was included along with the Washington Hat, the London Hat, and the thirty-three-foot high San Francisco Hat. The director of the de Young had the idea for the show, and he asked Silver to curate the exhibition because he thought the show would "loosen up the image of the Fine Arts Museums and open up a new audience." And he was right—the show was a huge success.

Spending two months curating the show, Silver said of the venture, "I never throw anything away. It was an adventure to plunge back into time, to get reacquainted with the bulk of crepe paper, cardboard, tape, and plastics; and then to have to essentially edit my life in terms of determining what to include for display. It was rejuvenating and exhausting at the same time." Silver

spent an afternoon with the docents of the museum, educating them about his artistic visions. Even the chairman of docent training wrote him a note of gratitude: "You gave us so many wonderful anecdotes and amusing situations that will help to enliven our tours for the public. The costumes, hats, and other objects certainly convey that delightful incongruity that you mentioned. *Beach Blanket Babylon* has probably given more joy and won more friends for our city than any other event."

The show made both adults and the young-at-heart giggle, but when a teacher from the Sutro Children's Center wrote to Silver to let him know how the exhibit had really touched the preschoolers, he was especially delighted. Evidently, the pre-kindergarten class was so taken with the display of *Beach Blanket Babylon* hats and costumes that their teacher decided to have her class construct their own "very big hats."

Sands
DUNES
ALADDIN
CAESARS
PALACE
RIVIERA
DESERT INN
GOLDEN
NUGGET
CIRCUS CIRCUS

CHAPTER FOUR

From Babylon to Vegas

STEVE SILVER'S APPROACH TO SCRIPTING THE SHOWS WAS A GENUINE DEPARTURE FROM THE DRAMATIST'S USUAL METHOD. "I WRITE WITH PICTURES," HE ONCE EXPLAINED. AFTER DRAWING EACH SHOW BY HAND HE WOULD USE THE ILLUSTRATIONS TO EXPLAIN THE CHARACTERS TO THE CAST, CREATE THE COSTUMES, CHOOSE THE MUSIC, AND DEVELOP THE DIALOGUE.

STEVE STRIVED TO MAKE EVERY INCARNATION OF *Beach Blanket Babylon* BETTER THAN THE LAST. THE PRIMARY *Beach Blanket Babylon* STORY LINE IN WHICH SNOW WHITE SEARCHES FOR LOVE ENDURES TODAY, ALTHOUGH OVER THE YEARS SILVER OCCASIONALLY INTRODUCED OTHER MAIN CHARACTERS INCLUDING DOROTHY FROM *The Wizard of Oz* AND THE "NERDS." HERE'S A TIMELINE OF THE MOST INNOVATIVE AND FABULOUS SHOWS IN *Beach Blanket Babylon* HISTORY.

Beach Blanket Babylon
at the Savoy Tivoli

WHEN AUDIENCES FIRST SAW THE PREMIERE edition of *Beach Blanket Babylon*, in the tiny back room of the Savoy Tivoli, the floor of the small North Beach cafe was spread with sand, oldies-but-goodies music was blasting overhead, and bikini-clad waitresses took drink orders and danced in the aisles. A lifeguard operated the lights seated on a tall lifeguard platform at the back of the theater. The ushers gleefully sprayed audience members with suntan lotion while Silver was backstage gluing sequins on costumes and adding last minute touches to the show.

When the show started, four French poodles played the overture, followed by two large M&Ms singing a duet. A fifteen-foot ocean wave parted revealing Nancy Bleiweiss in a billowing, pink-spangled cloud singing the "Sempre Libre" from *La Traviata* in a shrill, deadpan soprano, following it with a Connie Francis hit. Mary-Cleere Haran's re-creation of Rita Hayworth singing "Put the Blame on Mame" was terrifically sexy. When younger sister Eithne accompanied her on stage dressed exactly like Haran to sing a duet, the audiences went crazy!

Beach Blanket Babylon at the Olympus Club

AFTER THE SUCCESSFUL RUN AT THE SAVOY TIVOLI, *BEACH Blanket Babylon* opened at a nightclub called The Olympus. It was billed as "America's Bisexual Show-place," but it attracted everybody; and since the show was clean as a whistle from start to finish, you could take your youngster to see it. *Beach Blanket Babylon* was paired with a performance by the yet-to-be famous female impersonator Charles Pierce, and *Beach Blanket Babylon* quickly established a word-of-mouth cult following and earned wonderful reviews. The show was expanded to ninety minutes and was tighter than ever. It was a tribute to summer sun and beach party movies that only Silver could invent. The unlikely potpourri of characters included Santa Claus, Christmas Trees, surfers, and take-offs on Glinda the Good, Rita Hayworth, and Carmen Miranda. With five tap-dancing Christmas Trees soft-shoeing to "Me and My Shadow" accompanied by a four-piece orchestra dressed in white poodle costumes, it is no wonder the show was a hit. Four beach boys ready for the sun with zinc oxide on their noses and clutching surfboards served as the male quartet for the show, and each actor was given a chance to shine. The lunacy was wilder than ever, and the talent equal to the job.

© Al Hirschfeld

Beach Blanket Babylon Goes Bananas at Club Fugazi

WHEN SILVER ACQUIRED HIS LONG LEASE at Club Fugazi, the sixty-three-year-old North Beach landmark building, the tightly knit Italian community was pleased to support the opening of his entertainment venture. *Beach Blanket Babylon Goes Bananas* was an expanded version of the former show, and Silver added more characters with defined personalities. Glenda Glayzer, dressed foot-to-head in blue, sang a rousing rendition of "Am I Blue" and Lynn Brown, dressed as a gorilla, did a very funny striptease to Cole Porter's famous song "Night and Day." The talent was apparent to all, and the backdrops on the stage were wonderfully inventive, changing from an enormous postcard reading "Greetings from California" to a huge pineapple, or the crotch and front pockets of a pair of Levis, or a large eye with a teardrop.

Beach boys with surfboards, girls clad in water lily costumes, big game safari hunters, M&Ms, and apes singing "I'm Goin' Out of My Head" holding their heads in their hands, made the crowd go bananas. One journalist said, "If Flo Ziegfeld was around, he'd buy the whole show, from poodles to pineapples, and ship it off to New York."

75

Beach Blanket Babylon Goes to the Stars at Club Fugazi

Silver backstage with crew members.

THE HALLMARKS OF THE PREVIOUS SHOWS WERE ALL there in *Beach Blanket Babylon Goes to the Stars,* but this time the theme was show biz. The character of Snow White made her debut in this show, played by Penny Hamilton, who was described as "moving like an animated Swiss wind-up doll and sounding like Minnie Mouse." The production begins as Snow White tiptoes into Schwab's Drugstore looking for her Prince and hoping to be discovered, like Lana Turner. From then on, the show embraces every cliché in show biz, from the MGM lion to the Academy Awards. Armistead Maupin, of *Tales of the City*

fame, wrote much of the dialogue, and his one-liners added the proper Hollywood punch.

It wasn't just the audiences who had a few laughs during the show. Bill Kendall, whose parody of John Travolta in *Saturday Night Fever* was a scene stealer, was the perfect target for the off stage antics of the stage crew. Every evening, during the few moments when Kendall would glance stage left before assuming his Travolta pose, the crew tried to make him laugh—but despite their efforts, Kendall never flinched. Until the night when the crew convinced Capp, the owner of Capp's Corner, the restaurant next door, to aid them in their quest. That evening when Kendall glanced backstage, he saw Capp—with his trademark cigar hanging out of the corner of his mouth—holding a plate of steaming pasta. Kendall just couldn't keep his pose, and, trying not to laugh, barely sputtered the first lines to his song, "Staying Alive."

Kendall, who died from AIDS at age 35, was an integral part of the show, originating the enduring characters of Mr. Peanut, Superman, and a perfect John Travolta. On February 20, 1988, Silver dedicated The Bill Kendall AIDS Research Center at the University of California at San Francisco in his honor.

Beach Blanket Babylon Goes to the Stars and the Beach at California Hall

FOR THE SEVENTH ANNIVERSARY OF *BEACH BLAN-KET Babylon*, Silver successfully convinced his heroine of the beach-blanket movies, Annette Funicello, to be his honored guest. The show he envisioned was so big that he decided to launch his tribute to her, *Beach Blanket Babylon Goes to the Stars and the Beach,* in a larger theater at California Hall. Importing, among other things, eleven tons of sand, beach umbrellas, and even authentic hot dog stands, the surf was up. Ms. Mousketeer, in her best surfer form, was a smash. She clearly enjoyed her newfound *Beach Blanket Babylon* fame and it was a feather in Silver's cap that he was able to persuade the reclusive Funicello to appear. She had all but retired from show biz. Years later, Silver would again salute her and her on-screen partner, Frankie Avalon.

Beach Blanket Babylon Goes to the Stars and the Beach continued to receive rave reviews, without Funicello, and after the summer run at California Hall, the show returned to Club Fugazi and continued for four more months before the next version was introduced.

Left to right: *Bill Kendall, Annette Funicello, Steve Silver, Michael Ashton (kneeling)*

Beach Blanket Babylon Goes to the Stars and Broadway

BEACH BLANKET BABYLON GOES TO THE STARS AND *Broadway* was a fitting tribute to the genre that Silver loved so much, and even the often hard-to-please New York critics loved it. One critic from the *Village Voice* said, "Beach Blanket is explicitly about San Francisco, and although it pulls its share of the tourists, it's been kept alive by the local audiences. It's such a piffle that I have an embarrassing confession—I really enjoyed it. Seen on its own turf, Beach Blanket can cajole a smile from the grumpiest Applephile. For its latest incarnation, *Beach Blanket Babylon Goes to the Stars and Broadway*, San Francisco dares to wave its tiny fist at New York."

In this production, Snow White searched for her Prince with Joan Crawford and Mama Rose from *Gypsy* serving as guides to the Big Apple. Silver exchanged Sardi's for Schwab's, and as Snow White searched for fame, employment, and true love, she encountered singing and dancing restaurant tables, Superman, Mr. Peanut, Annie, and other magical characters. Many critics called this incarnation of the show the best *Beach Blanket Babylon* to date. In January 1982, Jo Schuman saw Silver's show for the first time and thought it was brilliant. She was so impressed by Silver's creativity that it prompted her to write him a fan letter.

Beach Blanket Babylon Goes to Washington

WHEN HE WAS INVITED BY THE REAGANS to bring his stellar cast to the White House to perform for the politicos, Silver was overwhelmed with the possibilities for laughs. After all, what better place to stage a show about illusions than in a city filled with master illusionists? According to rumor, the official invitation was offered because Jerry Zipkin, a friend of the Reagans, saw the show and loved it. Herb Caen exposed the rumor in his column, "Jerry 'The Social Moth' Zipkin, Queen Nancy's chum, saw *Beach Blanket Babylon* here recently and just knew that Nancy and Ronnie would love it. Everybody loves *Beach Blanket Babylon*, even grumps who say they can't stand it."

Unfortunately, however, the show was abruptly canceled. Silver had spent a great deal of time and money preparing for the show, and he wasn't about to let it go to waste. He opened *Beach Blanket Babylon Goes to Washington* for a four-week run at Club Fugazi, which was festively decorated with flags and red, white, and blue banners. The duet "We're Goin' to the White House and We're Goin' to Redecorate It" by Nancy and Ronnie Reagan was the audience's favorite. The fabulously inventive White House Hat that appeared on Snow White's head during the finale had faithful replicas of Washington's most famous buildings: the White House, the Capitol, the Washington Monument, and the Lincoln Memorial.

Beach Blanket Babylon
Goes to London

STEVE SILVER AND HIS PAL CHARLOTTE MAILLIARD SWIG were responsible for writing the show that was indeed fit for a Queen. When Her Royal Highness Queen Elizabeth and Prince Philip visited San Francisco, the pair had their work cut out for them. Preparing a seventeen-minute version of *Beach Blanket Babylon* was no simple feat, but their tribute to the visiting royalty was successful. The Queen was so delighted by the performance that she requested a photograph of Mr. Peanut (Bill Kendall), since the character apparently bore a resemblance to a member in her Cabinet. When the finale hat appeared, Prince Philip became ecstatic. He couldn't get over the enormous London Hat, which showed Buckingham Palace (complete with marching guards), the Tower of London, and a Big Ben tower that opened to reveal photos of the Royal Family. When Silver found out that the Queen called her visit to San Francisco the high point of her trip to the United States, he was delighted.

Beach Blanket Babylon Goes to the Prom

WHEN THE SHOW WENT TO THE PROM TO CELEBRATE ITS tenth anniversary, Silver pulled out all the stops. Marking the show's 3,300th performance, *Beach Blanket Babylon Goes to the Prom* was a party to thank all those in the community who had supported the show for the past decade. Surrounded by ten searchlights sending beams across the sky, the guests walked down a balloon-decked, red-carpet path to be greeted by a squad of cheerleaders from the mythical *Beach Blanket Babylon* High School. The Riordan High School Band played on one side of the entranceway, while the San Francisco Gay Freedom Day Marching Band was on the other. Silver had arranged for the city to close the street in front of the club (now called Beach Blanket Babylon Boulevard) for the evening, and complimentary wine and champagne flowed freely. Guests could even have their official prom pictures taken by a photographer on hand.

After the evening's performance, Silver took to the stage and thanked his guests for their support. Addressing the audience with heartfelt appreciation, he told them, "Everyone here is special to me, and this room is full of love." And he meant it. It was a fête that San Francisco and Silver would long remember.

Beach Blanket Babylon Makin' Whoopee

WHAT BETTER EVENING THAN VALENTINE'S Day to premiere the newest *Beach Blanket Babylon, Makin' Whoopee*, the first program without Snow White. Instead, a pair of "nerds" played by Susan Parks and Bob Kastanek adventure to find true love.

Silver took a chance on changing his main character, but it didn't sway the critics' attitudes one bit. Bay Area arts reporter Barbara Bladen wrote, "Silver is a genius. He sticks with the tried and true, even down to closing every show with his surefire signature song, 'Happy Trails to You,' and the ever popular 'San Francisco, Open Your Golden Gate' as the Transamerica Building rises 15 floors higher on Diamond's yard-wide hat. Surely, you've seen it. Haven't you? Well, shame on you. Everyone else on your block has."

Beach Blanket Babylon
Goes Around the World

was in need of a back-up it was a grand excuse to hold "doggie auditions." Over fifty-seven canines and their owners turned out, and in this (pardon the expression) dog-eat-dog business of theater, it made for a highly unusual casting call.

Beach Blanket Babylon Goes Around the World continued for almost four years and Silver's highly evolved Around the World Hat was a big hit.

IN MARCH 1986 SILVER SWITCHED THE MAIN CHARACTER from the "nerds" to Dorothy from *The Wizard of Oz*. In the show Dorothy searches for love and finds herself all over the map, in Rome, Paris, London, and once again in San Francisco, meeting The Boss (Bruce Springsteen), Dr. Ruth, King Louis XIV, Tina Turner, the Queen of England, Mary Poppins, and Prince along the way.

Always the promoter, Silver even staged auditions for her co-star Toto. Silver intended to use Cyril Magnin's dog Tippy Canoe in the show, but since he

Above: *The 4,000th performance of the show was given in honor of two of Silver's favorite entertainers, Carol Channing and Mary Martin. For the occasion, the two legends placed their palms and signatures in wet cement for future exhibit in front of Club Fugazi.*

Beach Blanket Babylon: Las Vegas

THROUGH THE YEARS, Silver received many offers to take the show to various cities, but it wasn't until the cigar-smoking executives at the Sands Resort and Casino offered him a terrific opportunity that he became interested. Silver had always wanted to play Vegas. While *Beach Blanket Babylon Goes Around the World* flourished in San Francisco, Silver tailor-made a new program to suit the desert's sensibilities that was full of hilarious references to gambling, show girls, and other Vegas trivia. He held auditions in Los Angeles and hired a separate cast for this production. In Los Angeles, Silver met his protégé and current artistic director for the show, Kenny Mazlow. Mazlow, an incredibly talented and versatile performer, appeared during the entire Las Vegas run. Silver hired him to join the San Francisco cast after that engagement.

Decorated like a South Sea Island, the Copa Room of the hotel was turned into a beach with palm trees, beach balls, towels, a lifeguard stand, and tons of sand on the floor. The audience could get into the spirit by digging their heels into the sand; after all, it was the Sands hotel. It was a smash hit in Vegas town. Writing for *Dramalogue*, Lee Melville said, "Steve Silver is bringing something unique to Las Vegas with his special version of *Beach Blanket Babylon*, a satirical and outrageous revue that is approaching its 15th anniversary in its hometown of San Francisco, which is quite a different city from the capital of glitz and kitsch nearly as renowned for its T&A as its slots and gambling tables. But Las Vegas has never before encountered this Silver, who is brighter and more resilient than its silver dollars (and more genuine, too). Showmen come and go in Las Vegas, and while most of their entertainment wares have had little substance, hidden behind sequins and feathers, Silver's ingenious fun is out in the open (and he doesn't have to display nudity to catch the eye)."

Beach Blanket Babylon's Twentieth Anniversary

IN THE TWENTIETH-ANNIVERSARY SHOW, held in the gorgeous San Francisco Opera House, over one hundred people shared the stage wearing eighty-five hats. Silver asked Frankie Avalon and Annette Funicello, the king and queen of the beach-blanket films, to be his guests of honor for the evening, which benefited the AIDS Memorial Grove in Golden Gate Park and the city's New Main Library. Each organization received a check for $100,000 from Silver. Tommy Tune flew in from Los Angeles to introduce Val Diamond, and she was joined by other cast members from previous productions of the show. Shelly Werk performed her wonderful "Life Is a Cabaret" skit, à la Liza Minnelli; Penny Hamilton, the original Snow White, sang excerpts from *Gypsy;* and the standing-room-only audience was deliciously sur-prised when Charles Pierce, who once shared the bill with *Beach Blanket Babylon* in the early days, appeared on stage. Four-year-old Melody Travers, whose mother had auditioned for Silver, sparked Silver's interest when she accompanied her mom to the audition. He was so impressed he hired her for this performance and this little belter-to-be brought the house down with her version of "Let Me Entertain You." The crowning point of the evening, of course, was the spectacular three-hundred-pound San Francisco Hat. The show was a never-to-be-forgotten celebration of everyone's favorite and long-est-running theatrical revue, and another high point in Silver's life.

In 1990 the show returned to its original title of *Beach Blanket Babylon,* which it retains to this very day, and although Silver is no longer among us, every effort is made to preserve his wishes for the show's future and to preserve and continue his legacy.

© Al Hirschfeld

85

The Oscars 1989

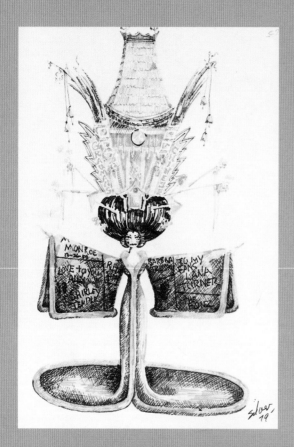

and tables and the massive six-hundred-pound hat of Grauman's Chinese Theater weren't shot very effectively. Silver had lost artistic control, and although the cast had a terrific time in Los Angeles, the performance was a mess in more ways than one.

When Snow White (Eileen Bowman) sang with bad-boy actor Rob Lowe in the opening act, *they* were not amused. *They* in this case was The Disney Company, which was unhappy with a parody with one of their characters that was appearing on television without the company's permission. Other viewers were amused, one famous fan in particular. Former President Ronald Reagan even called the producer of the show, Allan Carr, to tell him how much he loved it. "I used to go to the Coconut Grove to watch the Oscars. It was the best television show I've ever seen."

The opening number and the ensuing controversy has since become legend, and Silver, characteristically, transformed the

One of Silver's dreams come true was to stage the Academy Awards, and in 1989 he had his wish, although it didn't exactly work out as expected. Asked to stage the opening number for the Oscars, Silver was delighted. But the production was a critical debacle that had little to do with his original vision. The directing for this show was less than perfect, and the camera angles failed to enrich the *Beach Blanket Babylon* touches. The dancing stars experience into a great opportunity to laugh. Years later, during a special *Beach Blanket Babylon* Oscars party, a cigarette-lipped, down-and-dirty Snow White (played by Kenny Mazlow) appeared screaming, "Steve, you ruined me!" Of course, it was all in good-natured fun. And, good-natured fun was what *Beach Blanket Babylon* was and is all about.

Right: *In 1993, Silver and his wife, Jo Schuman Silver posed in front of a Grauman's Chinese Theater character.*

CHAPTER FIVE

Nothing Is Sacred

THE TRADITIONS OF PARODY AND BURLESQUE IN LEGITIMATE THEATER HAVE A LEGACY THAT DATES BACK TO THE EIGHTEENTH CENTURY IN EUROPE, WHEN AUDIENCES WOULD FILL UP FAIRGROUNDS AND SMALL PLAYHOUSES CLAMORING TO BE ENTERTAINED. AND ALTHOUGH SILVER'S SHOW DEFIES DEFINITION BY MOST STANDARDS, IT DRAWS ON BOTH OF THOSE TRADITIONS, ESPECIALLY PARODY; BUT IN *Beach Blanket Babylon*, THE PARODY NEVER STINGS. THERE ARE MANY REASONS FOR THE SHOW'S SUCCESS, SUCH AS ITS USE OF FIRST-RATE TALENT, INSPIRED LUNACY, AND SKILLFUL REPARTEE, BUT THE SHOW'S GENTLER USE OF PARODY IS ALSO AN IMPORTANT ELEMENT. *Beach Blanket Babylon* IS A DEPARTURE, FROM THE TYPICAL NIGHTCLUB REVUE IN WHICH VULGAR LANGUAGE, CRUEL JOKES, AND BATHROOM HUMOR IS THE RULE, NOT THE EXCEPTION.

The modus operandi of parody is to "make fun of," and often the resulting satire is mean-spirited. But *Beach Blanket Babylon*'s use of parody in dialogue and visuals has an innocent quality. The nightly audiences always comprise a mixture of ages and cultural and geographical backgrounds. Everyone finds the show funny, which is no mean feat; and *Beach Blanket Babylon* wouldn't be as successful as it is without its universal silliness. Imagine trying to get over three thousand people a week to agree on what is funny!

Steve Silver's approach to parody was always to "have fun with," never "make fun of." For example, in *Beach Blanket Babylon Goes to the Stars and the Prom*, a chorus of East Indians dressed in dhotis with white turbans on their heads sing and tap dance to "I'm a Yankee Doodle

Gandhi," and then they segue into a Michael Jackson number, "Feel It," a take-off of Jackson's hit, "Beat It." Silver's use of visual and literal puns, the nonstop energy of the production, the complete absurdity of the material, and the outrageous costumes and headdresses combine to create a spectacular entertainment that celebrates pop culture in general and the city of San Francisco in particular.

Who else but Silver would create Barbara Bush—literally—as a bush with a string of pearls and a white curly wig? Or his wonderful Tina Turner character, tressed with tufted hair as high as the sky? Or a

Left and Above: *The Love Boat Hat, worn by songstress Val Diamond, was a terrific parody of that long-running television show. Silver's attention to detail is apparent when you compare the sketch and the finished product.*

The two songs that always

end the *Beach Blanket Babylon*

show are "Happy Trails to You"

and "San Francisco." Roy Rogers,

Dale Evans, and Jeanette Mac-

Donald would be proud.

⋆ ⋆ ⋆ ⋆

scene with two animated cigarette boxes, Kool and True, singing "Smoke Gets in Your Eyes." The visual aspect of the parodies is what makes them work so well, whether the show is lampooning Elvis, Carol Channing, Mary Martin, John Travolta, Eva Peron, Sly Stallone's Rocky, the Reagans, or *Miami Vice*'s Don Johnson. Show after show, the characters Silver chose to lampoon reflected who was in the news or a current icon of popular culture. His genius lay not only in choosing the most talked about celebrity, but also in the manner in which he lampooned them. He had a second sense for selecting people from the worlds of politics, music, fashion, Hollywood—whoever might be currently enjoying their fifteen minutes of fame.

**Previous page, Left, and Following
pages:** *Pop and cultural icons from
past and present are the most popular
celebrities lampooned. After all, their
larger-than-life status just begs for a
moment on the* Beach Blanket
Babylon *stage. Here are a few of
them: Joan Crawford, the Flying
Nun, Sonny and Cher, the "We Are
the World" group (Willie Nelson,
Cyndi Lauper, Bruce Springsteen,
Tina Turner, Stevie Wonder),
Madonna, Elvis, Tina Turner,
and Prince.*

According to Armistead Maupin, novelist and former writer for the show, "He [Silver] saw the absurdity in modern commercial and popular culture and figured out a way to point up that absurdity and make people feel good about it at the same time. The shows are savagely cynical and very sentimental all at once, and I think that's one of the reasons that *Beach Blanket Babylon* has survived all these years."

Using the heroes and heroines, both fallen and elevated, of the times, Silver had an intuitive sense for selecting the characters who would garner the public's attention. No one in the public eye was spared, and he loved to bring in political legends such as the British royal family or American presidents and their first ladies. Silver even added the character of Lady Di tap dancing to "Dixie" in one production. The jokes in the show aren't always jokes, but rather references to what is *au courant*. With a laugh line every ten to twenty seconds, there isn't much time to tell a joke, and the visual elements and song and dance routines must tell the story.

The 1986 "We Are the World" skit with Bruce Springsteen, Stevie Wonder, Willie Nelson, Tina Turner, and Cindy Lauper is an example of Silver's skill at parody. Who else *but* Silver could get away with parodying Stevie Wonder? The audience screamed with laughter at the line, "Does Stevie Wonder?" yet they were people who normally would never laugh at a blind man. Religion is another tricky subject to fool around with, but a scene in one show with bearded rabbis singing "Have a Tequila" to the tune of "Havah Nagila" as they danced around a stage set called Bar Mitzvah succeeded without offending anyone.

Sometimes the legends lampooned are a throwback to icons of the past, like the Village People, or Sonny and Cher—characters that have revisited the show decades after they first appeared. A Sonny and Cher skit, with Sonny as a SONY TV set and an over-the-top, long-limbed Cher belting out "Half-breed" unintelligibly is humor that endures.

© Al Hirschfeld

Opposite: *King Louis and Snow White.*

Silver worked closely with cast members in an effort to stretch their capacity as performers, and it brought out the best in each actor. In a field that more often concerns itself with "business" than "show," Silver was an exception. Artistic director Kenny Mazlow explained, "I think the one ability that Steve had that touched so many people was that he loved to find the potential inside of people. He had this imaginary shovel, and he loved to find the gold inside of a person. He would sit and talk with anybody. After you spoke with Steve Silver, you felt like you were a worthy human being with a special talent. He would dig inside and find the gold, whether it was creative or personal, and he would then make you *aware* of what that was and he would be there to nurture it. He made you feel important."

In the process of digging for that gold inside of his actors, Silver would often put his cast on the edge. Relying on their talents and quick thinking, he frequently delighted in giving cast members dialogue just moments before they were to appear onstage. On several occasions, he gave Val Diamond new dialogue. Ignoring her protestations, he insisted that she could do it, and of course she did.

Silver loved to be entertained, and he never got tired of inventing and re-inventing the show. He was fond of extracting "over-the-top" elements from his actors and would-be actors, and he offered them the opportunity to go even further than *they* thought they could go. During auditions for the show, he would rely on improvisation and sometimes he would ask professional classical music singers to sing like Prince, or Cher, or their Uncle Sid. Hundreds of people would show up for the auditions, which frequently lasted ten to twelve hours. Although it was clear that, with a ten-member cast, only a few people would make the final cut, Silver was always courteous and respectful, even when the talent quotient of some of the auditioners was quite negligible. During the auditions, Silver looked for specific qualities. "A good voice is the most important thing. What I look for in auditions is not sparkling eyes and lots of teeth, but that special something—something unique that's peculiar to that performer—and I spot how to make that quality work. Sometimes no one else might see why I cast so-and-so, but I know I can use it in the show. Whole routines will emerge as a result of that one special quality."

Opposite and Above: *Over the years, Beach Blanket Babylon has used Liza Minnelli's Sally Bowles character in Cabaret countless times. The results have always been hilarious, whether it was with one Liza or four. Notice the real Liza Minnelli backstage with the Silvers (Steve and Jo) and some of the cast members.*

New Main Library

The Steve Silver *Beach Blanket Babylon* Music Center, constructed in honor of the impresario, is part of the San Francisco New Main Library. For three months beginning in April 1996, a special exhibit of *Beach Blanket Babylon* sketches, costumes, photos, and trivia was shown at the Library's grand opening. The press and public turned out in huge numbers, and the exhibit was a fitting tribute to Silver's madcap talents. Miniature models depicted some of the most famous *Beach Blanket Babylon* hats. The music room in his honor stands to inspire other impresarios-to-be in the town he loved so much.

Silver's attention to each auditioner was legendary, and he would push them, urging them to give it their all. During one audition, he told some of the semifinalists, "All of you have great voices. I'm trying to see how far you can go in characterizations or accents so you can really let yourself go." The kindness that Silver extended to the hundreds who did show up was returned by many letters from auditioners who didn't make the cut. One letter stated, "A belated thank you for your patient direction of

the *Beach Blanket Babylon* auditions. I really appreciate the courtesy you showed to the performers. I also really enjoyed watching all the other auditioners—a show in itself! Looks like I'm on the four-year plan, so I'll see you at the next round." Another woman who was invited to attend the auditions as Silver's guest wrote, "If I ever have to be rejected, I hope it's by Steve Silver."

Beach Blanket Babylon endures, and there is every reason to believe that the show will not only go on,

Above: *Backstage, Silver prepares for* Beach Blanket Babylon Goes Around the World.

but thrive through the next century. For fourteen years, Jo Schuman Silver worked closely with Silver on various *Beach Blanket Babylon* incarnations. It was little wonder that after his death, he left his show to her, knowing that she would maintain and adhere to his creative vision because she understood it so well. He's a tough act to follow, and there is now a committed group, with Schuman Silver at the helm, that guides the show. This group includes general manager David Lincoln King, artistic director Kenny Mazlow, stage manager John Camajani, and the multi-talented Val Diamond. Team play has always been part of *Beach Blanket Babylon.* Alan Greenspan, who has spent almost two decades making hats for the show, describes it as follows: "It's a wonderful thing being connected with the show in any way; it really is. When I meet

people who ask me what I do for a living, I love to tell them I work for *Beach Blanket Babylon*. It's special; and any connection to it, whether you work in the box office or play in the band or are a cast member, is a remarkable thing."

Schuman Silver promises to keep that spirit alive. "*Beach Blanket Babylon* is definitely a team and a collaborative effort. We are all working together to continue the legacy of Steve Silver." In the future, it is quite possible that *Beach Blanket Babylon* may be coming to a theater near you.

Above: *Prop expert Bill Jones and Silver team up on the King Kamehameha costume.*

Awards and Charities

Silver never lost sight of the city that was so supportive of his work. He was a philanthropist, and in 1993, he created the Top Hat Awards to honor performers he believed contributed the most to the entertainment world. Recipients included Tommy Tune (1993), Frankie Avalon and Annette Funicello (1994), and Carol Channing (1995). Monies donated by *Beach Blanket Babylon* were used to purchase special items for the community or to promote a cause. When Tommy Tune received his award (right), Silver donated a piano with a plaque bearing Tune's name to the High School for the Performing Arts in San Francisco. When the beach party couple, Frankie and Annette, were saluted, Silver donated $100,000 to the AIDS Memorial Grove in Golden Gate Park. He also made a donation to build a Music Center at the San Francisco New Main Library. When Carol Channing was saluted with a Top Hat Award, he donated sets of orchestral-quality tympani drums to Lowell High School, both Channing's and Silver's alma mater.

Silver gave back to the community that supported him so much. He donated hundreds of thousands of dollars to charities, including Project Open Hand, the *Beach Blanket Babylon* Pediatric Playroom at the California Pacific Medical Center, the Sonoma Valley High School Awards for Promising Artistic Talent in the Arts, iron gates to the Shakespeare Garden in Golden Gate Park (in honor of Cyril Magnin), the *Beach Blanket Babylon* Child Development Center at Parent's Place, the Cancer Research Lab at the UCSF Medical Center, lighting for Washington Square in San Francisco's North Beach, the AIDS Emergency Fund, and several hospice gardens.

Community involvement and charitable activities remain an essential part of *Beach Blanket Babylon*.

> *"Farewell, dear Showman Steve, and may angels sing and dance and make merry for you eternally in heaven."*
>
> — GEORGE CHRISTY, *The Hollywood Reporter*

FARLEY *Phil Frank*